GEOFFREY BEST is dean of the School of European Studies at the University of Sussex.

To no group subject to sociological and political analysis has honour seemed to matter more than to the military. Their idea of it has commonly been accepted as the most superior, open to emulation to the limited extent that different circumstances and purposes in non-military life permit.

The degeneration of this concept and of the public realm in which honour's obligations have to be observed is the subject of this book, based on the 1981 Joanne Goodman Lectures at the University of Western Ontario.

Best begins with the discovery, in the age of the American and French revolutions, of the nation as the supreme object of honourable service. He discusses how nationalism and democracy marched together through the nineteenth century to harden this creed and broaden its base, so that what had previously been a code for noblemen became a popular code for patriots.

He finds that, in spite of the historical naturalness, even inevitability, of nationalism, its ensuing and corrective counter-current, internationalism, is a much more appealing principle. In internationalism, a tradition of cosmopolitan, transnational thought and activity, unmoved by the passions of nationalism and critical of them on the grounds of humanity and peace, he perceives a greater field for honourable service – honour's obligation to the service of mankind.

Best casts new light upon some familiar historical episodes and values and suggests fruitful fields for future study.

THE JOANNE GOODMAN LECTURES

Delivered at The University of Western Ontario

1976
C.P. Stacey
Mackenzie King and the Atlantic Triangle
(Toronto: Macmillan of Canada / Maclean Hunter Press 1976)

1977
Robin W. Winks
The Relevance of Canadian History:
U.S. and Imperial Perspectives
(Toronto: Macmillan of Canada 1979)

1978
Robert Rhodes James
Britain in Transition

1979
Charles Ritchie
Diplomacy: The Changing Scene

1980
Kenneth A. Lockridge
Settlement and Unsettlement in Early America:
The Crisis of Political Legitimacy before the Revolution
(New York: Cambridge University Press 1981)

HONOUR AMONG MEN AND NATIONS

Transformations of an Idea

The 1981 Joanne Goodman Lectures
GEOFFREY BEST

University of Toronto Press
Toronto Buffalo London

© University of Toronto Press 1982
Toronto Buffalo London
Reprinted in paperback 2014

ISBN 978-0-8020-2459-6 (cloth)
ISBN 978-0-8020-6472-1 (paper)

Canadian Cataloguing in Publication Data

Best, Geoffrey.
  Honour among men and nations

  (The Joanne Goodman lectures ; 1981)
  ISBN 978-0-8020-2459-6 (bound). − ISBN 978-0-8020-6472-1 (pbk.)

  1. Honor. 2. Nationalism. 3. Internationalism.
  I. Title. II. Series: The Joanne Goodman memorial
  lectures ; 1981.

  JC328.B47   320.5   C82-094520-X

The Joanne Goodman Lecture Series

has been established by Joanne's family

and friends to perpetuate the memory of her

blithe spirit, her quest for knowledge, and

the rewarding years she spent at the

University of Western Ontario.

Contents

Foreword

The Joanne Goodman Lectures were established at the University of Western Ontario in 1975 to honour the memory of the elder daughter of Mr and Mrs Edwin A. Goodman of Toronto. Each year the university invites a scholar to deliver three lectures on some aspect of the history of the English-speaking peoples, particularly those of the Atlantic Triangle of Canada, the United Kingdom, and the United States, that will be of interest to members of the university community and the general public. The list of those who have so far participated in the series indicates the distinction of these lectures and the part they play in the intellectual life of the institution. The University of Western Ontario is grateful to Mr and Mrs Goodman and their family and friends for this generous and moving benefaction dedicated to a student who loved history and enjoyed her years at this university.

Professor Geoffrey Best, dean of the School of European Studies at the University of Sussex, has long been acknowledged as one of the leading historians of Victorian religion and society. But by 1971 when he published *Mid-Victorian Britain 1851–1875*, the best synthesis and interpretation of the high point of nineteenth-century civilization, he was already greatly expanding and changing the range of his scholarly interests in a manner exemplary but daunting to other historians by turning to the history of modern warfare and the international law designed to regulate and temper its brutality. A decade of study has already resulted in one volume, *Humanity in Warfare* (1981), and we at the University of Western Ontario were fortunate in being the first to hear Professor Best's reflections on the changes and continuity in the concept of military honour from the aristocratic eighteenth century to the democratic, and totalitarian, twentieth. The warmth and ebullience of his personality, his concern for and passionate championship of humanity, and his hopes for the future in a solemn hour for such prognostications left a lasting impression on those who heard the lectures and shine through this permanent record that can be shared with a wider audience.

Neville Thompson
The University of Western Ontario

Preface

The idea for the lectures on which this book is based dawned on
me during my many years of work on the modern history of the
international law of war. Exactly how it relates to that theme,
and how it too springs from certain personal preoccupations, is
loosely described in the opening paragraphs of the first lecture. It
seems desirable here to add a few introductory words about the
nature and limits of this very selective scrutiny of the idea of
honour in relation to the history of nationalism and internationalism – even, perhaps, an explanation of how it relates to
it at all.

Honour being such a protean concept, capable of many social
and personal applications, it must at once be said that the application central to this story is the military one. To no group subject to sociological and political analysis has honour seemed to
matter more than to the military. Their idea of it has commonly
been accepted as the most superior idea available, open for emulation and copying by others to the extent – the limited extent, it
has most often been understood – that the different circumstances and purposes of non-military lives permitted. That honour in however debased a form is still somehow central to
soldiering was sadly recalled to me when, not long after delivery
of the lectures, I saw in the World Council of Churches' film

Revolution or Death recruits of the El Salvador army drilling to shouts of 'Honour is our motto.' Such degeneration of a once-noble concept, noted from time to time in these pages, parallels within the military (a profession committed more than most to the values of its past) the complication – in some ways also, it must be said, a degeneration too – of the public realm within which honour's obligations had to be observed.

Therein lies the larger context of this book: the history of nationalism and its opposite and corrective, internationalism. To what gods was the man of honour bound to dedicate himself? Whom or what did his code of honour oblige him to serve? The heart of the story told in these pages is of the discovery, in the age of the American and French revolutions, of the nation as the supreme object of honourable service; perhaps co-equal with the monarch (undisputed supreme object up to then) but in the most striking cases above him or in his place. Nationalism and democracy marched together through the nineteenth century to harden this creed and to broaden its base, so that what had previously been a precise code for noblemen became a popular code for patriots: 'the nationalization of honour' having among its products the concept of 'national honour,' the importance of protecting or avenging it, the extension to the nation as a whole of the old personal preference of death to dishonour, and so on. Nationalist rhetoric has changed little since the generations of Brissot, Fichte, Decatur, and Mazzini. The language with which they sought to stimulate the energies of their compatriots has become familiar to our generation through the mouths of all who seek to defend, liberate, or avenge nations still.

Nationalism, as must soon become obvious to readers of this book, does not much appeal to me. It is much more questionable than patriotism. The historical naturalness – even inevitability – of it the historian in me cannot deny. Nor can I in good conscience wish to falsify a record which includes, besides so much personal nobility and heroism, nothing less than the making of the political map of the modern world. Yet the record, if it is to be faithfully represented, includes also that corrective counter-current of, to put it briefly, internationalism: a tradition of cosmopolitan, *trans*national thought and activity, relatively unmoved by the passions of nationalism and consistently critical of them on broad grounds of humanity and peace; appealing, so to speak, from mankind drunk to mankind sober. To any dispassionate observer, nationalism must seem fearfully ambivalent. I cannot conceal my preference for this alternative principle, nor the acuteness of my anxiety lest the unrelenting surge of nationalist passions should undo even the small progress made by internationalism since the Second World War. Part of that progress has been the discovery or, as it seems to me, rediscovery of an international or transnational field for honourable service; honour's obligation to the service not of one nation, but of mankind, humanity at large; a still unexhausted theme and prospect, with which this story comes to its end.

The critic may at once observe that the story told here is a strictly selective one, beginning arbitrarily about 1770, ending arbitrarily about 1960, and leaving out of account an enormous amount before, during, and since. The critic will be right. The last thing here laid claim to is completeness. The best thing the author can hope to have done is to have demonstrated some connections not heretofore too obvious, to have cast upon some very familiar historical episodes and values a not-so-familiar light, and to have suggested to the research-minded some fruitful fields for future study. The Postscript briefly sketches what some of them might be.

All that remains to be done now is to express my gratitude to the University of Western Ontario for inviting me to deliver the 1981 lectures in the Joanne Goodman Lecture Series. The text of this book follows closely those lectures as they were delivered on 10, 11, and 12 March 1981, differing only in such predictable ways as including some detail which then had to be omitted for reasons of time and in being supported now by endnotes and by the addition of a Postscript. Not only was it an honour and privilege to be allowed to give the lectures; the giving itself was made extremely pleasant by the generous welcome and hospitality of Mr and Mrs Edwin Goodman, of the president of the university, and of friendly members of its faculty, notably Professors Neville Thompson and Peter Neary.

The assembling of material and pursuit of clues relative to such an unusual and potentially unwieldy topic have led me to take advice from several friends and colleagues over the past eighteen months. I am glad of this opportunity to thank Mr Sydney Bailey, Dr Joan Beaumont, Mme Renée Bédarida, Mr Peter Calvocoressi, Dr Charles Carrington, Mr David Chandler, Mr Michael Donelan, Dr Christopher Duffy, Mr Owen Dudley Edwards, Professor John Erickson, Dr Paddy Griffith, Professor Norman Hampson, Professor James Joll, Dr Paul Kennedy, Dr Piers Mackesy, Dr Barrie Paskins, Professor John Pocock, Professor John Röhl, Mr Andrew Wheatcroft, Dr Philip Wigley, Dr Rupert Wilkinson, and the librarians (and their staffs) of the University of Sussex, the Institute for Advanced Legal Studies, and the Ministry of Defence.

Finally, I must say how blessed I have been in the tactful support and speedy work of the secretary to the dean of the School of European Studies at the University of Sussex, Mrs Barbara Garrett. That a beloved wife has been indispensable, too, hardly needs to be added.

Geoffrey Best
Dean of the School of European Studies
University of Sussex

1

Noblemen
and
the Rest

WHEN THE DECISION was made to honour me with an invitation to give the 1981 Joanne Goodman Lectures, it must have been expected that in giving them I might not depart wholly from the preoccupations of the last ten years of my working life. They have been to write a history of the international law of war: those evolving codes of prohibitions and restraints, the Geneva Conventions the best known of them, by which States have attempted to limit the material and psychological damages of their deadly quarrels.[1] That work had frustrations as well as fulfilments. Partly because I sought to write it within a compass and in a manner that would not deter the general reader, partly because I more and more realized that the choice before me was to publish an imperfect book now or a perfect book never, and partly because there could only be arbitrarily set barriers between my story and that of the general history of war, I found myself having continually to pass by cognate matters that seemed to be at least as interesting as the one to which alone I could give my full attention. All I could do was to salute them in passing, pin fragments of some of them in a footnote or two, and hope to return to the more manageable of them when opportunity offered. Such an opportunity arrived with the invitation to give these lectures. In them I am going to explore some aspects of an idea which I found repeatedly in many forms across my path: the idea of honour.

Before we get to it, however, it is necessary to visit for a few minutes the common source of that earlier work and this, and to disclose my personal interest, as I believe all scholars should do if it may have something to do with their choice of topics for study. I did what I did then and I do what I do now mainly because of a frightened fascination with the problem of violence – violence in self and society, violence in the relations between political societies – and the whole spectrum of explanations men give themselves about it. And I explain my own approach, in part, as that of an Englishman and a European in his fifties. People who seek to explain things historically must accept the risk of being explained historically themselves. My Europe was a continent ravaged and divided by war: wars so habitual throughout its history that most people know its history as one of wars and little else, a habit of wars that culminated in the total ones of 1914–18 and 1939–45. It was understandable enough that each of those dreadful conflicts should have been followed by urgent attempts to defuse the nationalisms which seemed to have been so largely responsible for them, to integrate the nations' interests in some new and safer way, and to review from the foundations upwards the received wisdom that war was probably desirable and certainly inevitable. It was understandable also that the attempts after the First World War having achieved so little, those after the second should have been more extensive. The United Nations Organization performed upon the same stage as the League of Nations but with a larger cast and in some hope of embodying not just internationalism but, beyond it, universality. Of more immediate consequence to my corner of the universe was the urgent concern felt in all parts of it, as the war ground to a halt, to cure the continent at last of the malaise which had now proved so nearly suicidal.

Out of that concern came the movement for institutional reform which produced, in 1951, the European Coal and Steel Community and, in 1955, the EEC proper: a radical reform of the continental States-system, designed to denationalize it and to bring about in its half of Europe what the United Nations no doubt would take longer to bring about globally, some pioneer measure of supranational organization. In the aftermath of the war, such a hope did not seem vain; and the historian of Europe may in due course discover, what for me is only an impression, that that hope has faded with the shrinking of that proportion of western Europe's population which had experienced war at first hand.

With that unique political side of Europe's search for salvation from the recurrence of war, we need have little more to do.

Closer to our theme, and indeed directly introducing it, is the
more psychological side, seeking the roots of international conflict in the cultures and mentalities that sustained the States
themselves and had something to do with their habits of mutual
hostility. Exactly how much, remains problematical. All who
look seriously into the great question of the causes of war agree
that in some sense, as is proclaimed so prominently in the
United Nations building, war begins in the mind;[2] people only
differ as to how much of it can be said to begin anywhere else. In
contrast to its political inventiveness, Europe has proved to be no
pioneer in this branch of war and peace studies. Between the
wars indeed they made more of a showing in the United States
than anywhere else. But Europe has caught up since 1945. The
undiminishing flood of war-loving books, war-glamourizing art,
and war-fomenting talk, which has grown *pari passu* (I reckon)
with the revival of nationalism since about the end of the fifties,
is at any rate accompanied by the endeavours, scholarly and
imaginative both, of a host of persons desirous to remind a for-
getful world of the darker side of war, and to impede the building-
up of that mood of acceptance and expectation of war known in
the conflict research business as 'war psychosis.' Nothing can be
much deeper in the mind, I suppose, than psychosis, and the
difficulties of curing it must seem formidable to anyone who
recognizes it as something to be cured. Yet people in Europe as
well as in North America speak boldly of changing mental habits
hardly less ingrained; the way men of one colour have, for
example, of distancing themselves from men of another, or simply man's way of regarding woman as more of an object than an
equal. While anyone really hopes to abolish racism and sexism,
let no one denounce the abolition of war as unrealistic.

To argue against war and all recourse to violence is intelligible
enough, and in the mouths of its most thoughtful advocates
considerably persuasive; but it is a religious or an ethical argument, not any sort of scientific one. The bulk of the critical analysts of war to whom I have referred and among whom I

modestly class myself are possessed more with the idea that war-lovers have had it too much their own way than with absolute rejection of war itself. Because they find evidence to suggest that war's realities are largely repulsive, its costs often frightful, and its causes sometimes insignificant, their interest is to point up aspects which its devotees have neglected and which might make some of them think again. Tending to believe that war has happened too often and too easily, they interpret this as a re-proach to mankind, but they do not generally suppose that it may be easily or completely got rid of. Some at least of them conclude, however heavy-heartedly, that war is sometimes neces-sary and sometimes justified. Without meaning any disrespect to the conscientious pacifist, they wish things could seem as simple to them as presumably things do to him. Instead of pure prin-ciple, *for* war or *against* it, they have to live with dilemmas and paradox. The path they have to tread is the thin and thorny one of admitting that the use of force may be justified between States (as it is certainly justified as a last resort for maintaining public order within them), while calling attention to the probability that on *these* historical occasions it was much less justified than on *those*, and on *that* occasion seems not to have been justified at all. Writers ready to draw such distinctions about wars them-selves will draw them also about the states of mind which brought those wars about, discriminating as best they can be-tween the virtuous and the ignoble; they will not let their recog-nition that war brings out some of the best in men blind them to the fact that it also brings out some of the worst. They will be on the watch for the multiple mythologies and emotional trip-wires which operate to discourage inquiries such as theirs. They even choose to discuss notions like, for instance, honour.

At once you will wish to know, within what definitions and limits is this great concept going to be discussed? Certainly we must know exactly what we are up to, or the theme of honour will smother us all. It is a giant, and a familiar giant, in the mighty band of concepts commonly invoked to justify or control human behaviour. It has entered into most amazingly wide employment. Early in schooldays we learnt to tell truth, or to keep secrets, 'on our honour.' Pre-military service in what used to be called Boy Scouts and Girl Guides, Wolf Cubs and Brownies, was soaked in the idea. Teenage boys were adjured to respect the honour of teenage girls, and the latter were urgently advised to guard it. 'Honour thy father and mother,' begins the Fifth Commandment in the King James translation of our Bible. The traditional Anglican rite according to which my wife and I became formally attached to each other twenty-six years ago required of me the undertaking to 'love ... comfort ... *honour* and keep her,' and of her the undertaking that she would 'obey ... serve ... love ... *honour* and keep' me, so long as we both should live. The younger sons of peers in Britain are titled 'Honourable'; members of Parliament and a host of other public officials should be addressed, by anyone who wishes to get it exactly right, as 'the Right Honourable.' Old-fashioned businessmen may still express concern for 'the honour of the firm'; soldiers even of the newer fashions are expected to do anything 'for the honour of the flag' and 'the honour of the regiment.' To be precise, they are expected to be ready to die for it. Honour, though no doubt less frequently on the lips of people in the 1980s than it was before the moral earthquakes of the 1960s, retains in its more elevated and refined uses the very high ethical value it has in fact always and everywhere had of something proper human beings value so much that they must prefer it to mortal life itself. It or something very like it is to be found in all major religions and cultures, testifying at least to its general acceptance as a rare and precious virtue – sometimes the highest of them all. Wherever men help women and children to escape from danger before they do, captains are last to leave the sinking ship, and pilots stay on the crashing plane to steer it clear of houses, wherever people

keep their promises to tell the truth even at disadvantage to
themselves, honour is at work, helping the actions which excite
admiration, on the one hand, and on the other, causing us to
know and admire them as 'honourable.' Civilization, we might
well think, would be the poorer for its absence, and the moral
potential of mankind so much the less.

But unfortunately it is not quite as simple as that. For the awkward fact is that this attribute of man in some of his best aspects
can also appear in some of his worst. What is often taken to be
the noblest aspect of honour, that it has power to summon men
to brave death rather than live in dishonour, needs only a slight
turn of the ethical prism to become questionable. Was the cause
for which they died actually a good one? Was it worth it? Did it
deserve such tribute? One may argue endlessly about the ethics
of self-sacrifice. The ethics of making sacrifices of others may
perhaps be dealt with more summarily. Codes of honour, so-
called, have been and still may be responsible for much of that.
Some cultures make more of honour than others. Duelling with
swords or pistols has given way, in Western societies, to boxing-
gloves, libel actions, the lampoon, and the letter to the newspaper. European and North American husbands no longer feel
obliged to kill wives who have merely *appeared* to be having
affairs. But women may be numbered in hundreds of millions
whose menfolks' conventions of honour still require all kinds of
female servitude and suffering; wherever the blood feud and the
vendetta persist, honour is by definition at a premium; what
does the organization known among its own people and in its
own territories as 'the honoured society' turn out to be but the
Mafia? Let us take a close-up of Mafia man in 1861 Sicily. 'With
his low forehead, ornamental quiffs of hair on the temples,
lurching walk and perpetual swelling of the right trouser pocket
where he kept a knife, it was obvious at once, that Vincenzino
was "a man of honour," one of those violent cretins capable of
any havoc': thus Giuseppe di Lampedusa's approach to our

theme in one of the greatest novels of our century.[3] Honour and its twin-concept duty have formed a familiar shield for crooks, bullies, hypocrites, and paranoiacs, of one of whom Emerson observed: 'The louder he talked of his honour, the faster we counted the spoons.'[4] George Bernard Shaw's summary of the matter was: 'When a stupid man is doing something he is ashamed of, he always declares that it is his duty.'[5]

One does not need to be as cynical as that to recognize the reality of our problem. The idea of honour, great and ennobling in many familiar applications, becomes vile and base in others. It stands for something far too important to men, apparently (though perhaps not to women), to be dispensable from their behavioural vocabulary, and it is something which seems to be a necessary part of the moral cement of virtually every society known to us; yet its objective content is extremely variable, and its applications are not uniformly admirable. It has a high capacity to make men die, but on its own it says nothing about any other reasons why they should be willing to die, and the men who professionally talk most about it may be unable to agree about what it requires of them. An air chief marshal last autumn maintained in a letter to *The Times* that the 'mole' who was leaking to the press from the Ministry of Defence reports of the service chiefs' opposition to budget cuts was doing an honourable thing. The most vehement rebuttal came from a lieutenant-colonel.[6]

This conveniently brings us to the particular strand of the history of this idea which I wish to explore. The concept turns up in all sorts of contexts and with infinite varieties of meaning; but its core in our culture, from which its spores have been, as it were, diffused through the rest of society, has always lain among the military. Whatever may be the whole explanation for that special connection, it obviously has something to do with special characteristics of the military life: its requirement of personal bravery, which men and women instinctively admire; its closeness to death, which men will not cheerfully risk without some very great compulsion; and its camaraderie, which places a high premium on loyalty and sacrifice. Yet those integral ties to soldiering and sailoring are not enough to explain the virtual military monopoly of honour which we find in Europe at our starting point about two centuries ago. Bravery might be shown, death be defied, and comrades in arms supported by 'other ranks' as well as officers; but only officers were deemed to possess honour, and only among officers and their kind was the military code of honour known and respected. It was, in fact, the prerogative of a class and a caste: the nobility, to give the general European phenomenon its accepted title; officers and gentlemen, in a classic English formula. 'The British army is what it is,' wrote the Duke of Wellington, the greatest of our soldiers, 'because it is officered by gentlemen: men who would scorn to do a dishonourable thing and who have something more at stake than military smartness.'[7] Officers and gentlemen are still with us, and the classic conception of honour is still alive and well among them; but their military monopoly of it has long been broken. The 'other ranks' have become eligible for its distinctions, just as the rest of society has (less successfully) demanded its opening to them as well. These intensely interesting transformations are part of modern social history, and their particular story fits into that familiar one of the erosion of aristocratic privilege and exclusiveness by ideas of democracy and equality. But it goes beyond that. It is also a part of the history of politics and political thought. The political applications of the soldier's honour have undergone transforming enlargement too, and therein lies the other, perhaps darker, side of our theme. Men fought for their countries consciously enough before the American and French revolutions gave them a new vocabulary for explaining why they should do so, but the prevailing code of honour held something higher than the interest of the country. Patriotism was not enough for the men who knew the most about it; and since they – the aristocratic military élite of Europe in general – controlled the whole of State policy, led the fighting, and set its tone, their feelings had considerable public weight. How far they or any other social group were 'nationalists' before the French Revolution remains open to debate. It can in fact be quite difficult to determine where patriotism ends and nationalism begins. How, for example, should we label the late Elizabethan mentality projected by Shakespeare on to 'old John of Gaunt, time-honour'd Lancaster'?

This royal throne of kings, this scepter'd isle,
This earth of majesty, this seat of Mars,
This other Eden, demi-paradise,
This fortress built by Nature for herself
Against infection and the hand of war,
This happy breed of men, this little world,
This precious stone set in the silver sea,
Which serves it in the office of a wall,
Or as a moat defensive to a house,
Against the envy of less happier lands,
This blessed plot, this earth, this realm, this England.[8]

What patriotism has ever been more exalted than that put into the mouth of John of Gaunt's great-nephew Henry V beneath the breach at Harfleur – 'Cry, "God for Harry! England and Saint George!"' – or on the morn of Agincourt:

We few, we happy few, we band of brothers;
For he today that sheds his blood with me
Shall be my brother; be he ne'er so vile
This day shall gentle his condition:
And gentlemen in England now a-bed
Shall think themselves accurs'd they were not here,
And hold their manhoods cheap whiles any speaks
That fought with us upon Saint Crispin's day.[9]

By some definitions of nationalism, the English (dodging for the moment an awkward question, by counting the Scots and Welsh as honorary Englishmen) never properly experienced it at all but went straight from an unusually national sort of patriotism to an unusually imperialist sort of nationalism, which was, however, as the official title of the Empire and Commonwealth indicates, British, not English.

What the British inherited from so much history that they did not have to bother about the theory of it, the French, Germans, Italians, and continental others, not to mention the new-born Americans, had to invent in passionate haste when revolution hit them about the end of the eighteenth century. However scholars define nationalism and classify its varieties, there is consensus as to the novelty of the nationalisms which then flooded through so many continental European people, with such momentous consequences for their history then and ever since. The consequence that concerns us is what all this did to honour. In a word, it nationalized it; in the process and outcome, popularizing, democratizing, and vulgarizing it. 'National honour' became an expression to conjure with in the nineteenth century, and what it conjured up had much to do with aggression, xenophobia, and militarism. We encounter again the phenomenon of a concept intrinsically rich in moral grandeur running into uses the most diverse and dubious. President Carter and President-elect Reagan rang many changes on 'the honour and dignity of the United States' in their protracted dispute with Iran about the American hostages, and one may perhaps think it merely unfortunate that the Iranians' use of exactly the same concepts did much to prevent their coming to an accommodation. But what is one to think when one meets it in – to mention some recent cases, randomly noticed – President Kim Il Sung's announcement that upholding North Korea's 'dignity and honour' was a prime condition of his Ten Point Policy; the new United States secretary of state, at the same time as he down-

graded human rights, expressing his objective as 'a strong America working with honour and grace'; and ex-President Idi Amin Dada's thirst to restore 'dignity' to Uganda? Is 'vulgarization' strong enough a term?[10]
It was all much simpler and more exclusive before the deluge. There is our starting point, when the fabric of the *ancien régime*, although it revealed perilous cracks to the probing eye, still stood intact, and within it the kind of honour we are most concerned with, the soldier's, meant something relatively precise and particular. It was primarily an attribute of the nobility, the aristocracy, the gently born and bred. Of course, reflections and echoes of it were to be found at all levels of society, if only for the reason that men are emulative and the distinguishing marks of accepted hierarchical élites are always to some extent copied or paralleled lower down. So much was this the case in the monarchies of the *ancien régime* that one of the acutest sociological analysts of them, Montesquieu, concluded that honour was the moving spirit and characteristic moral cement of monarchical systems of government in general.[11] He did not wholly approve of it, but as a pioneer social scientist he observed that it worked and as a man of principle he had no doubt that monarchies, with all their faults and foibles, were preferable to despotisms and to anarchy; and of monarchies, orders of nobility were the natural prop. Among noblemen honour was most naturally at home. It was through their kind that our central strand of honour had directly descended from earlier ages and it was by them, in each successive generation, that it was articulated into precise social forms and usages. The rest might ape and borrow, even criticize. In the most economically dynamic countries the nobility might have to share with some of the richer of the rest their privileges and their style; in the United Provinces, in Great Britain, and to a smaller extent in France, for example, the blood-purity of nobility had become adulterated, and the borderlines between it and the rest in varying degrees blurred. But the border stayed secure

even there, and in no department of life was that border more peremptory than in the military one.

You will recall the simple summary of feudal society: peasants did the work, priests and monks did the praying, and noblemen did the fighting. We may recall also Karl Demeter's terse explanation of chivalry: 'Siegfried became St George.'[12] Fighting in due course became too big and complicated a business to be done any longer just by noblemen and their retinues, but it was still led by them, it continued to dominate the minds and lives of many of them, and – what matters most for our purposes – the honour that came with it was appropriated by them. Nowhere was the distinction between noblemen and the rest sharper than here, and nothing showed it more than the place honour had in their mentalities. For except where it was the custom to regard the rank and file as mere robots, scarcely human, it was not denied that the rest were capable of good fighting qualities: courage above all, but also devotion to duty, loyalty to the group, obedience to orders, and perhaps patriotism too. To our later-twentieth-century minds, this might seem enough for any man. But it did not, for the *ancien régime* ruling class, include honour in the extensive way that Shakespeare had let it do for his Henry V. The honour that mattered now was something else: the complicated code of behaviour on and off the battlefield by which men of the class indoctrinated with the conviction that they and their sort alone were capable of it recognized each other, no matter whose side they were fighting on. The rest fought under the orders of their king's officers for their king and country; officers and gentlemen fought also for honour's sake, and by honour's peculiar rules of what was right and proper to do, what was undoable and unthinkable. King and country were not quite all in all to them. Their order was transnational, so was their code of honour, and so also, therefore, were the compulsions that led them into armed service and to be ready to die. They might find no higher satisfaction than in going to death for the sake of honour, and after their death honour would be done to them, perhaps in other countries as well as their own. But the deaths of soldiers outside the officer corps were of less interest in their own countries, and could of course be of no interest anywhere else. 'All is lost but Honour!' was actually exclaimed by the French king, François premier, after his defeat and capture at Pavia in 1525, but it came from the heart of this ancient tradition and would still be held in high respect wherever that tradition survived.[13]

One particular element of that tradition is the supranational self-sufficiency to which I referred in my remark that for the aristocratic military élites who led the international wars of the *ancien régime* the code of honour was most highly valued as a perfect end in itself. Such, certainly, was the language often employed by its devotees. How much did it really mean? It is important for my argument that it meant something in political terms as well as social. The social meaning is much the more obvious, and I shall have said almost enough about it when I say 'duelling.' This familiar concomitant of old European nobility was entirely and centrally to do with honour, but no public interest could be seen to be served by it except in the romantic eyes of those who thought the practice helped maintain a high tone of honour, courage, skill at arms, and so on among society's natural leaders. Monarchs repeatedly tried to stop it, on good public grounds that it was contrary to Christian principles and, so far as the officer corps themselves were concerned, damaging to their cohesiveness and destructive of valuable lives. Literature lost Pushkin early, through a duel; how many budding Bonapartes went that way too? But it persisted almost everywhere, largely because of the utterly non-utilitarian caste-conscious principle at the root of it, that honour was its own thing, with imperatives that trumped all others.

Much less conspicuous than duelling but much more significant in the history of honour's transformations is its political implication, that proper respect for it may clash with public policy or with orders received. One dares not make too much of this, partly because little research seems to have been done on it.[14] It must be admitted that an honour-conscious officer's sense of honour could as well lead him to obey an order his intelligence or morality questioned as steel his resolve to disobey it. Conscientious officers have always been liable to impalement on these alternative spikes. But in some military cultures, clearly, and at some epochs, the tide flows less strongly towards unquestioning absolute obedience than at others. For officers of the *ancien régime* there existed room for moral manoeuvre. In the Prussian army, for example, which under Frederick II had an unmatched reputation for discipline and obedience, it was nevertheless widely held among his officers that their honour entitled them to refuse to obey an order whose substance or style ran counter to it. As in respect of duelling, kings' attitudes towards this varied; to Frederick William I it seemed wholesome, to his son dangerous; the latter tried to stop it but even he could not purge the corps of so profound and congenial a conviction, and it persisted well into the nineteenth century.[15] Montesquieu explained it thus: 'There is nothing so strongly inculcated in monarchies, by the laws, by religion and honour, as submission to the prince's will; but this very honour tells us that the prince never ought to command a dishonourable action, because this would render us incapable of serving him.'[16] The example he cited came, like most of his examples, from an earlier age – from 1572, to be precise – but he could have found them in his own century. The Prussian General von Saldern, for instance, seems to have been thus motivated when he refused to obey Frederick the Great's order to wreck, by way of retaliation or revenge, the Saxon monarch's hunting lodge at Hubertusburg.[17] Close kin with the moral or religious delicacy that led an officer to decline to obey a dishonouring order was that which led him to avoid implication in dishonouring actions, and even to resign if he could not. Such scrupulousness was urged upon officers as no less than their conscientious duty by the respectable English clergyman Thomas Gisborne in his *Enquiry into the Duties of Men in the Higher and Middle Classes of Society in Great Britain*: 'The obedience which is the duty of an officer is prompt and punctual obedience to *lawful* authority. This ... implies that the thing commanded must be lawful; for otherwise the authority which presumes to enjoin it is so far unlawful. Were an officer then directed by his superiors to do what is contrary to the received laws of war and of nations; to the laws of his country; or to the laws of God; his compliance with that order would be criminal.'[18] How representative this was, it is impossible in the present state of research to say. But Gisborne's several instructional books went into edition after edition; he was not a crank or a nobody, any more than he was an original thinker; what he wrote must have sounded fairly reasonable. Disapproval of the principles for which the war had been undertaken caused certain British officers to decline to fight against the rebels in the Thirteen Colonies. The devious politics of the governor-general in India twenty years later led General Sir Arthur Wellesley, not quite yet the world-famous Wellington, to complain that they were in danger of sinking Britain's honourable reputation for plain dealing: 'I would sacrifice Gwalior, or every frontier of India, ten times over, in order to preserve our credit for scrupulous good faith, and the advantages and honour we gained by the late war and the peace ... What brought me through many difficulties in the war, and the negotiations for peace? The British good faith, and nothing else.'[19] His peer Colonel Walpole 'not only refused a sword of honour ... but resigned his commission' when the Assembly of Jamaica broke the faith Walpole had established with the Maroons whom he had induced to surrender and instead of letting them stay in the island sent them to Nova Scotia.[20]

Only the previous year some large part of the French revolutionary army turned a deaf ear to the National Convention's decree that no British and Hanoverian prisoners should be taken. It was not just the promptings of humanity that moved them, it was also the traditional code of honourable conduct which had come into their army with its pre-revolutionary professionals and which tended to be at its touchiest when (as in each of the examples I have given) it was rubbing up against *politicians*. The politicians who passed and sought to enforce that decree – the Jacobins – were, as a matter of fact, of special significance to our theme, as embodying the most direct and abrupt rejection of the values of the *ancien régime*. It would be convenient and tempting to try to argue that *ancien régime* honour disappeared from the Jacobins' world as completely as they wished. It did not, in proportion with the failure of their ambition totally to transform that world. But from their time onwards it had new and tougher enemies to deal with.

The Jacobins gave extreme expression to the movement of thought which had long been subjecting the *ancien régime* to critical scrutiny, and turned out in the end to be revolutionary. With only one item in that catalogue of ideas are we concerned: its rejection of the inherited honour system.[21] The criticisms, taken together, rejected it root and branch. Fastening particularly on to the 'artificialities' of aristocratic society – its elaborate social rituals and etiquette, its multi-layered mannerism, the premium it put on wit, malice, irony, and smoothness of discourse at the expense of plainness and truth – they stigmatized it as a kind of social upas tree, poisoning the manners and discourse of every other part of society which came into contact with it and, in *ancien régime* circumstances, aped it. Knowing their Montesquieu as well as we today know our Marx and Freud, the critics decided that, if this was what a socio-political system founded on honour was like, they wanted no part of it. The nobleman's honour in their eyes was tainted by the conventional immoralities which it was wont to cover: duelling pride, extravagance, and vice. The critics were never closer to unison than when denouncing the moral corruption – as they chose to perceive it – of the old order, the degeneracy of the times they found themselves living in and wanted to get out of. Their minds moving most easily around the literature of antiquity, more of a common culture to them than the Christian Bible, they held up for highest admiration societies like Athens and Sparta while they were still independent and republican Rome before its citizens became corrupted by dictators and prosperity. The exemplary excellence of those societies they attributed to their relative simplicity, naturalness, and austerity, and to their particular cultivation of *virtue*. Virtue was the quality they admired above all and strove to recover for mankind; virtue both personal, as a principle and ideal of private behaviour, and social, as the governing idea of good citizenship and inspiration of public conduct. Montesquieu had declared virtue to be the characteristic principle of republics, as honour was of monarchies. For his part, he preferred the latter, and showed little interest in the possibility that they could be replaced by anything better. The proto-revolutionaries, as we might call them, tended to be more rash, hopeful, and doctrinaire. The conversion of absolute monarchies into constitutional ones, which seemed to the moderate Anglophiles to promise to bring about most of what they wanted, could not appear as more than a mere beginning to men who had conceived of the new-style heaven on earth of a citizens' republic governed by virtue. Towards the end of 1792 they got their chance. *Virtue* was emphatically their watch word, mainly because they objectively believed in it and meant the enormous amount they wrote about it, partly because it was tactically necessary in order to distance themselves from the rival principle of honour, of which Montesquieu had made, and aristocracy continued to make, so much. But although republican doctrinaires preferred not to use the word, the substance of it of course never ceased to be coveted and respected among the military, and every other social group to whom peer judgment mattered. Replacing an honour-based monarchy by a virtue-based republic was for most mere reformers a very remote aim, if it was an aim at all, and a much lower priority than prising open the inherited honour system and democratizing it. This was the truly popular side of the critique of the *ancien régime* in Europe. Privilege and distinction were no longer to be inherited but to be earned. Society might still be arranged in ranks – hardly anyone seriously believed in practical equality – but they should be rationally explicable ranks (thus ran the liberal revolutionary mind) according to social or personal value, if indeed the two did not coincide. And man should still be capable of honourable distinction, but it would be distinction according to merit such as was within any man's capacity for showing.

This was, in a nutshell, the general revolutionary theory of later-eighteenth-century Europe. The exact terms in which it presented itself, the freedom with which it dared to express itself, varied vastly from country to country. What was publicly barely thinkable in St Petersburg, and barely mentionable in Berlin, was the talk of the town in Paris, House of Commons commonplace in London, and taken for granted all down the coast from Maine to Georgia. Whether men really meant what they said about liberty and equality, the nation and the people, and so on – how far they had thought about the implications of their rhetoric – was another matter. When revolution actually came, 'liberty' often turned out to mean my liberty to take advantage of you; 'the people' often meant simply the bourgeoisie. But honour, a value more detached from immediate economic and political practice, had more fixed a meaning. It meant the natural right of every man to earn, if he could, his society's highest esteem; and the field of endeavour in which he was most likely to be able to do so was, inevitably, the military one. Honour was already comfortably at home there. Well before 1789 military radicals everywhere were canvassing schemes for making armies more national, in the sense of becoming more representative of the people at large, or at any rate of the people who mattered. Such a prospect attracted them for three reasons, all lodged well within the general corpus of revolutionary thought. First, they argued that it would be better militarily. Officers whose minds had escaped from the fixed categories of aristocratic conservatism were experimenting with blueprints for acclimatizing the ancient model citizens' army in their own Europe. While their inflexibly backward-looking comrades stood by their ideal of a rigidly disciplined army raised no matter how, led by an honour-monopolizing élite, the reformers depicted the advantages of armies more homogeneous in social tone and dependent for discipline not just upon the sergeant's stick and the officer's sword but upon the patriotic spirit and home-defending enthusiasm of a citizen soldiery. Such an army would, they believed, not only be capable of adequate discipline but be much more likely to bring dash and valour into its fighting. Second, it would be safer politically. Professional armies of robotized riff-raff or semi-savage frontiersmen, led by an officer corps owing peculiar loyalty to a hereditary absolute monarch, were just about ideal for protecting privilege and oppression. A free people's liberties would be much safer if its armed force were in its own hands. And third, such a force would be more appropriate nationally. New, deep meanings were being read into the words *patrie, Vaterland,* and nation which presented armed service of them as man's sublimest joy and highest duty, a most honourable service, from which no self-respecting patriot should be barred. Military conservatives, suspicious anyway of the implications of popular political activity in these ideas, believed that this new wine could be contained in the old bottles, that the feelings of such socially respectable subjects as might have to be brought into the army would be sufficiently gratified by the honour embodied in their standards and their officers. Reformers were not sure that such so to speak vicarious participation would suffice, and the more they were touched by the revolutionary movement, the more did they feel sure that in any case it ought not to suffice. It seemed to them morally and politically wrong that men moved by patriotic zeal should not be free to fight for their country and to receive full honour for doing so. How far their thoughts went down the social scale or across the constitutional one depended, naturally, on character, time, and place. Whatever the ambiguities and overlappings in the middle bands of the spectrum of practice, the gulf now became unbridgeable between, on the one hand, the idea of honour which found it exclusively in the nobility and the snobbish officer corps which dominated it and carried their honour with them from service to this prince to service to that one and, on the other, the idea which attached it to the service of one country only, your own, and made it accessible to all subjects or citizens.

And so we come to the new national factor – new, that is to say, in the epoch of the American and French revolutions. I have already had cause to remark upon the difficulties of defining what exactly is new and what is not in the history of nationalism, and we must not pretend that things are simpler than they actually were. The rhetoric of patriotic service was as old as the Greek and Roman classics, and it was not impossible to believe 'dulce et decorum est pro patria mori' even in the Middle Ages.[22] What else but patriotic service was extolled in the Scotland of Robert the Bruce, the England of the first Elizabeth, the Holland of William of Orange? By the time of the Seven Years' War, patriotic military pride possessed at any rate parts of the populations of Great Britain, Prussia, and France. Edmund Burke and Jean-Jacques Rousseau – the British political philosopher who was to become the chief conservative hammer of the revolution, and the self-styled citizen of Geneva who was to appear as its chief theoretical inspirer – were extolling 'love of country' in similar terms several years before the revolution happened,[23] and the citizens of the United States, having set up a new country to love, set a cracking pace in showing how to do it. (It was not with the thought that George III expected every man to do his duty that

Nelson sought to stimulate the crews of his fleet on the morning of Trafalgar.) But none of this had in it the new depths of national meaning which were opened up by political revolution in France and cultural revolution in Germany.

Both found reasons why men should love their country and nothing else, and from both in due course came the unintended consequence that men should love their own country so much that they would have little love left for any other. The French Revolution did not begin like that. Its beginning contained much internationalism; it listened respectfully to idealists like Anacharsis Cloots, 'the orator of the human race,' proclaimed its generous love of humanity, and did not expect that anything more than its example and inspiration would be needed to bring about equally happy events everywhere else. But instead of copying it, the neighbours attacked it; love of humanity abroad needed to be backed by a reign of terror at home; internationalism turned into imperialism, patriotism into nationalism. The causes of such vast and rapid change lay partly in the force of circumstances and partly in the nature of political things, but they were also in part the product of the ideology of the Jacobin Club or (in modern terms) party. How much of that came from Rousseau, and through what channels, continues to be hotly debated. I take no position in that debate when I express this new-style nationalist ideology, for convenience's sake, in ideal Rousseauan terms. Rousseau valued the unity of the State above all things and maintained that the citizen should body and soul be bound to his State by what he called the general will and the civil religion, and what we can all recognize as national education. The idea of the general will of the citizens knocked the bottom out of theories of the State whose ingrained respect for minority or individual rights led them to limit sovereignty, or to balance powers; it boosted the credentials of the sovereign power to the maximum and it robbed the individual citizen of the right to say, about decisions of that power, that although he could not resist them, at least he had not been party to the making of them. By Rousseau's idea of it, he *had* been, which made dissociation from them the more awful. To this singular secular omnipotence, Rousseau's idea of civil religion added metaphysical force: 'a purely civil profession of faith, whose articles the sovereign is competent to determine ... without which it is impossible to be either a good citizen or a faithful subject. Without being able to oblige anyone to believe them, it can banish from the State anyone who does not ... banish him ... for being incapable of sincerely loving law and justice, and of sacrificing his life to his duty when necessary.'[24] Rousseau's republic had room only for the virtuous. The better to enlist men's beliefs ånd passions in the service of the State, Rousseau conceived the education of the nation in comprehensively nationalist terms. (Nationalist was not *his* word for it but we may properly use it, for that is what it turned out to be.) 'It is education,' he wrote, 'that must give souls a national formation, and direct their opinions and tastes in such a way that they will be patriotic by inclination, by passion, by necessity. When first he opens his eyes, an infant ought to see the fatherland, and up to the day of his death he ought never to see anything else ... This love is his whole existence ... he lives for [the fatherland] alone; when he has ceased to have a fatherland, he no longer exists.'[25]

While such an exclusive cult of the *patrie* was thus being fostered on one side of the Rhine, a somewhat different cult of the *Vaterland* was being fostered on the other. The French nationalism was always political, in its intentions, even before its revolutionary practice. German nationalism easily became even more political under stress of Napoleonic circumstances, but it did not begin that way. It began with historical and philological inquiry into the essence of German-ness, *Deutschtum*; and it discovered it in the manifold continuities, from earliest traceable times right up to the present, of the German *Volk*. The pre-revolutionary pioneers of this nationalism were not much worried by the manifold divisions of the German-speaking world. What interested them was recovering in all its depth and grandeur the great body of German culture, making it available for the inspiration and exaltation of the German spirit in the present, and building not less great achievement upon it in the future. Like French revolutionary sentiment before the Jacobin iron entered its soul, this too was internationalist, 'cosmopolitan,' but similar iron intruded not long after. In the effort of defending their Germanness against French hegemony, the leaders of German national sentiment discovered in their *Volk* a degree of separateness and exclusiveness which knew no equal. What marked it off from its great rival was its relative political moderation and what is best called its *Volkishness*, for no translation is quite satisfactory. There was much less basis and opportunity for political radicalism in Germany: fewer bourgeois, less wealth, especially in Prussia a much more functional and authoritative nobility, many more internal barriers and suffocations. A German revolutionary would only have seemed a mild liberal in revolutionary France. That does not matter to us. Volkishness does. It marked the beginning, for Germany, of something which was to become very dreadful for Germany and all her neighbours in our own generations, the proper translation of Hitler's use of the word *Volk* being 'race.' The equation was by no means so direct in the time of Goethe and Fichte, and in any case was innocent then of its later post-Darwinian resonance of biological determinism. But what it already had was resonant enough. 'Oh men of Germany!' cried a representative and very popular nationalist at the outbreak of their war of liberation early in 1813,

feel again God, hear and fear the eternal, and you hear and fear also your *Volk*; you feel again in God the honor and dignity of your fathers, their glorious history rejuvenates itself again in you, their firm and gallant virtue reblossoms in you, the whole German Fatherland stands again before you in the august halo of past centuries ...

One faith, one love, one courage, and one enthusiasm must gather
again the whole German folk in brotherly community ... No longer
Catholics and Protestants, no longer Prussians and Austrians, Saxons
and Bavarians, Silesians and Hanoverians, no longer of different
faith, different mentality, and different will – be Germans, be one,
will to be one by love and loyalty, and no devil will vanquish you.[26]

The intellectual sources of German and French nationalisms,
like the styles of rhetoric in which they were expressed, were
quite different, yet in relation to our theme their tendencies were
the same. In principle and in potential, they contained the
nationalization of values. In practice, they fell as yet far short of
such achievement. French national revolutionaries might yearn
to make all things new, but the French past persisted nevertheless, and under Bonaparte's eclectic direction they found much
of it glorious after all. German national patriots yearned only to
construct a safe modern structure for the spirit of their past to
inhabit and inspire. Among the orders of nobility and the military of both great nations, honour still held high sway, and liked
nothing better than to claim lineal descent from the heroes of the
past. Yet an enormous break had been made with that past,
whatever their unconcern about it or pretence that it had not
happened, a break whose consequences would irresistibly infil-
trate every culture within the Atlantic civilization which ran
from where Russia began to where Canada and the United States
ended. The new nationalism had driven a wedge between the
ancien régime's honour and its non-national points of reference.
Time would show how far that wedge was capable of being
driven.

2

Democracy
and
Nationalization

HISTORIANS OF NATIONALISM agree to differ in their estimates of how much of it (and what sorts of it) already existed in the Atlantic world of 1785. They are at one in recognizing that that world by 1815 was full of it, and that although each national variety had of course its own strong characteristics, those varieties had enough in common for it to constitute the most momentous phenomenon of modern history. And of its common elements, commonest was the relish of war. The peoples now becoming conscious (or perhaps just more conscious) of themselves as nations did so, without exception, in the course of armed conflict: fighting either to gain their independence from an alien ruler, as most obviously the Americans (whose example was much admired), the Belgians, Italians, Serbs, Greeks, and Poles; or to protect their independence against an invader, as the Germans, the Russians, the British, the Spaniards, and, at the beginning and the end, the French themselves. Whatever had previously been the martial and military content of national sentiment was now fortified and modernized. Each nationality in its struggle for independent survival acquired a brand new set of warrior heroes nicely adapted to its own needs and experience. Washington, Nelson, Ney, Blücher, Kutuzow, Espoz y Mina, Kosziusko, to name just representative singletons, came out of the mainstreams of their national cultures and so were very well suited to enrich them in their turn.

Towering over them all, of course, and in a class by himself, was Bonaparte. He was supremely representative of something different: the military spirit, pure and simple, and by general consensus martial genius as well. On those grounds, he commanded the admiration of war's professionals and connoisseurs irrespective of nationality. The success of his propaganda to the effect that he was a liberator and patron of oppressed nationalities, coupled with his undoubted success for many years in humbling their oppressors, also gave him a large transnational fame with most romantic revolutionaries. He was not so generally esteemed, we must remember, by real revolutionaries cut on the patterns of 1789 and 1793. That made him unique and peculiar among the warrior heroes of the age. Although the most celebrated of them, he was loathed by those among his own countrymen whose unbudging republican virtue enabled them to resist the glamour of the victories and conquests he placed at France's feet. The oppressiveness of his regime and the profligacy of his expenditure of young French manhood in fact made him domestically quite unpopular well before the end. Yet not many Frenchmen, it seems, had it in them to remain utterly untouched by all the honour and glory his armies brought them. France, after all, was by far the biggest military power in Europe, its martial tradition was as deep-rooted as any and (from 1792) was systematically cherished, much of the old royal army was carried over into the new revolutionary one, and Napoleon, in proportion as he gained power in the State, made it his business to make France's enormous army attractive to Frenchmen of every stripe, and succeeded. Pride in its achievements and love of its heroes were reinforced as central elements of a national tradition not so much broken in 1789 as restructured and reaffirmed. The glory, now, was freely shareable by all classes of the nation, just as was, for the most distinguished of them, membership of the Légion d'honneur he established in 1802. Better still, notable military service to the empire could bring nobility – not just the title but the income to go with it. The most favoured of his marshals and generals, some of whom had begun life obscurely enough, became princes and dukes; a mere drum-major, hastily produced in response to Napoleon's demand to meet the bravest man after a tough battle in April 1809, was on the spot made a knight of the Legion of Honour, a baron of the empire, and recipient of 4,000 francs a year.[1] This was eclecticism indeed! – honours and distinctions as before 1789, but available as awards and inducements to the nationally meritorious, whatever their backgrounds. To ideological purists, whether of the original revolution or of the surviving *ancien régime*, it made no consistent sense; but looked at in the light of militant nationalism, it made very good sense indeed.

With martial 'glory' thus proclaimed for universal admiration and military doings more widely known about than ever before and perhaps more highly valued, the code of honour remained as central and significant for the military as it had ever been, in apparently unbroken continuity from the past. Napoleon had enforced on the French and their satellites his unique amalgam of new revolutionary and old monarchical values, and something of the same sort happened by natural processes in the United States; the other armed forces of Europe, having experienced no revolutionary democratic upheaval, simply made such adaptations to post-revolutionary circumstance as their respective political developments required, which, in the cases of Russia and Austria-Hungary, for example, was hardly at all. The heart of honour thus still beat steadily within a scarcely disturbed military tradition. Yet there was more change than met the eye, and more than reflective military conservatives liked to reflect upon. We need notice them only briefly, because their serious effects were not to be felt till later.

First, the domination of officer corps by the old hereditary nobility had been weakened. Only in Prussia and the military empires of central and eastern Europe did it remain secure, and in Prussia only by dint of unremitting self-assertion. Elsewhere, bourgeois men and, what to the conservative aristocratic mind was worse, 'bourgeois values' broke in, most of all in France, whose officer corps henceforth never ceased to be the most openly recruited outside the United States. How far the men of self-conscious aristocratic values were justified in suspecting the lower-born of inability to observe the inherited code of honour, on the ground that you couldn't understand it unless you were born into it, is a question which cannot be gone into here. Advocates of bourgeois (even, sub-bourgeois) admission argued that what was functionally valuable in the old tradition would be absorbed by the new men, and what was not could be jettisoned. The professional military ethos being what it was, and class distinction and privilege proving as acceptable to most bourgeois as to all noblemen, it was not surprising that such absorption seems to have happened easily enough; either, as most significantly in Prussia, the nobility continued to prescribe the tone for the rest and the rest more or less gladly accepted it or, as most notably in France, the tradition was insensibly transmogrified into something which the newcomer could learn and absorb, and the workings of the institution itself would inculcate and enforce. Birth was not supposed to count for much in admissions to West Point, but none beat its graduates in devotion to 'Duty, Honour, Country.'

This brings us to the second and more serious shift in honour's circumstances. What country? Whose country? Such questions would have seemed silly, even perhaps wicked, to the ordinary earnest officer cadet at West Point and all its European counterparts in the early nineteenth century, but experience showed (what anxious conservatives had anticipated) that they could be very awkward questions indeed. Robert E. Lee and hundreds of other West Point graduates had to grapple with them in 1861. It is true that they might have prepared their minds for that grappling by reflection upon the possible implications of States' rights within the constitution of their country. They might also have recollected the revolutionary origins of their country's armed forces – when, after all, their founders had had to break their oaths of loyalty to King George. For British officers, who still took oaths of loyalty to a King George, no problem existed, it being universally understood that the king was 'the king-in-parliament' – a parliament whose control over the armed forces had long been complete. But for continental Europeans, the question posed itself differently, because honour's loyalty in the *ancien régime* was wholly owed to personal rulers. Officers may or may not have had 'country' in mind when they went to war. Their oath however was simply and directly to their prince, their liege lord. That oath was of extreme significance among men of honour. As I have already remarked, it established a personal or, one might say, family relationship with the prince, which was logically separable from the land he ruled, however much the two were normally identified in practice. When loyalty and service were due thus directly to a sovereign individual, their duty was absolutely clear to oath-bound holders of his commission.

Into this gratifyingly simple situation, the new national idea brought complications. Recognizing how naturally king and country ran together, the first French revolutionaries felt no difficulty about stretching the oath to cover both. Louis XVI took the new oath as he earnestly strove to move with the times. From one point of view, the liberal revolutionary one, a monarch could consider it positively flattering, popularizing, and strengthening to have his authority thus explicitly linked to the name and power of his people. Conservatives, however, did not like it, and wished he had not agreed so easily. From their point of view it weakened his authority. Revolutionary theory after all required monarchs to rule within the law of the constitution; conservatives could not avert their horrified gaze from the very visible arrière-pensée that a monarch who failed to rule to a people's satisfaction should be cashiered. The conservatives were quite right. Oaths of fidelity to king and country could only work satisfactorily so long as king and country stayed together. From the middle of 1791 they drifted apart, and the great majority of the French king's officers – men, of course, whose first oaths, before the deluge, had been taken to him alone – decided that it was with him that they should maintain faith, not with a patrie that was, by 1792, getting into very bad hands.

To have to make decisions like that was exceedingly distasteful to the gentlemanly officers of the French army. What their code of honour preferred was sharpness in ethical distinctions: the call of duty, clear and compelling; *this* clearly right, *that* clearly wrong. A man could face death in better heart when his conscience was easy. But for many of the armed services of Europe and North America such simple times were never to return. The *patrie* was here to stay, oaths taken to heads of State might seem to be incompatible with proper fidelity to the *patrie* and French officers would on several famous occasions have difficulty in making up their minds what it required of them. In 1814 and 1815 they would have to choose between their insatiably glorious but by now hopelessly defeated war-lord and their idea of a France restored to peace under different management. In 1830 and 1848 revolutions compelled them to choose again, nothing to guide them but their sense of what France demanded. So *la patrie* became the sole and exclusive object of their fidelity, no matter who was for the time being in charge, and this apolitical code of honour – patriotic and professional – served them well enough until they came to frightful grief in 1940, a matter to which we shall return later.

The problem was handled differently in Prussia and Germany. There, it could have become equally troublesome, had liberal constitutionalism been stronger. But Prussian crown and aristocracy survived in close enough harmony for the army to be saved any really awkward dilemma. Liberalism, during its first bold anti-Napoleonic flush, succeeded in enlarging the officer's oath to include 'the Fatherland' as well as the all-highest war-lord, but when in 1848 it tried to add 'the constitution' too, it failed; the officer corps absolutely would not hear of it, and Frederick William IV was soon dissuaded from his initial interest in it. That was the nearest they got to serious trouble before the end of the First World War. They felt a moral impossibility in imagining any distinction or difference in principle between king and country, and became indignant and angry when any other group within the State did so. Yet even upon the Prussian officer corps the possibility of having to make such a choice had been impressed on the penultimate day of 1812. The general commanding in East Prussia, von Yorck, took the, for him, gigantic mental step of deciding to pursue what he believed to be the national interest, instead of continuing to obey the orders of the king. Yorck and many other officers groaned under the weight and shame of the king's enforced servitude to Napoleon. When Napoleon's grand army was expelled from Russia and the Russians arrived in hot pursuit, Yorck, instead of resisting them as the king had politically ordered, concluded at Taurrogen a convention by which his Prussian forces were neutralized. This was soon followed by the king's escape from Berlin, denunciation of the French alliance, and general call to a war of national liberation. King and country were happily reunited, and the mainline of nationalist historiography trumpeted Yorck's decision as a brave doing on the king's behalf what the king would have wished, had he been free to wish it; in Rousseauan terms, divining the king's real will behind his actual will. But no matter how much noise monarchists made, the fact was that a senior general had done for the sake of his *Volk* what his king had not told him to do. Ancient precedents could be found for it, but it must have seemed a very modern-minded act to the minds of Stein, Scharnhorst, Gneisenau, Clausewitz, and the rest of the patriots burning to get at the French. *This* was what liberal nationalism, for them, was all about.

Yorck's interesting early example was followed more largely in 1848, by when was becoming more clearly articulated in the Prussian and other armies their most significant mode of reaction to the new nationalism: claiming to embody, even somehow to be, the essence of the nation, and peculiarly to represent its honour. While French generals, who had so much more politics going on around them, were coming to conclude that the course of honour was to keep out of the way, Prussian and Austrian generals felt obliged to take a more active stance. Those of them who made the greatest mark in resistance to the revolutions of 1848 did so by being more monarchical than their respective monarchs on certain crucial occasions – stretching orders, turning Nelsonian blind eyes to them, showing clear willingness to save their monarchs despite themselves, if they would not stand up and fight for their order, and so on. We here broach one of honour's biggest transformations. The tendency of armies to develop through the nineteenth century a sense of embodying not just their own honour but also that of the nation led to some extraordinary incidents, and gave a gratuitous handle to the anti-militarism whose own development was inversely geared to it.

Incidents could not be wholly unexpected in Germany. Germany appeared to be the military country *par excellence* in the late-nineteenth-century world, if prominence of army among national institutions, influence of army in national decision-making, and social standing of officers were any guide. Each former State within the German Empire had made its own contribution to the Kaiser's army, but the Prussian army was by far the largest and the Prussian officer corps dominated the whole. Most liberals and all men of the left disliked the social separateness of the corps, the insolence and arrogance of so much of its behaviour, the wall of social and actual privilege behind which its peculiar code of honour was able to continue to sanction a style of behaviour – the duelling, especially – considerably removed from that of respectable civil society. The officer corps' anachronistic offensiveness was only not more publicly troublesome because so much of German bourgeois society had actually become mentally militarized to the point where it was glad to be trampled on. Even so, there were, besides the trickle of domestic rows, at least two incidents grotesque enough in nature and grim enough in implications to command international attention. One, in 1906, was also funny. A down-and-out cobbler, Wilhelm Voigt, humorously revenged himself and all his kind on an authoritarian State which had never been friendly to them by donning the manner as well as the uniform of a guards officer and taking over the town hall of Köpenick, a Berlin suburb, for the day; quite accurately reckoning on the strength of habits of subservience to military presence. The Captain of Köpenick soon became an international figure of fun.[2] The other, in 1913, was less laughable: the culmination at what was then called Zabern but is now Saverne in Alsace of a series of rows between the populace and the military, revealing all too starkly the bullying mentality of the military and the ultimate inability of the civil authority, in Kaiser Wilhelm II's Reich, to protect civilians from it.

It was, oddly enough, another practical joke which brings the British armed forces into this part of the story. On 10 February 1910 HMS *Dreadnought*, flagship of the Home Fleet, being then at Weymouth, and having received notice by a telegram from 'the Foreign Office,' was distinguished by a State visit by 'the Emperor of Abyssinia' and suite. Everything went off perfectly. Only a few days later did the vanity of one of the party lead it to become known that the dusky dignitaries had actually been Virginia Woolf and three other bright young Bloomsbury-ites in fancy dress. Naval officers took it with awful seriousness: 'direct insult to His Majesty's flag,' 'insult to the honour of the service,' and so on. A group of young officers determined to avenge their sullied honour by thrashing the young painter Duncan Grant. All the steam went out of them when, having abducted him to a quiet spot on Hampstead Heath, they found he offered no resistance, the honour of the navy 'more than half defeated by the gentle perplexity and mild courage of a pacifist in carpet slippers.'[3]

Such incidents were significant enough of what national armed forces expected to get away with, or were allowed to get away with, in that feverishly nationalistic and imperialistic late-nineteenth-century world, out of whose self-destructive débâcle our own world was born. Each nation's culture having its own balances of the bellicose and the pacifistic in its mentality and of the civil with the military in its constitution, the degrees of special honour claimed by armed forces and conventionally accorded to them varied from land to land. In some countries that honour was actively protected by the law. It was considered as much of an offence to impugn that honour as it was to insult the flag.[4] How far such laws may still exist, I do not know; I recall however that newspaper men and popular comedians were prosecuted in Spain only three years or so ago for insulting the army, and I am credibly told that the honour they ascribe to themselves is one of the most jealously protected attributes of the military regimes of Latin America. Political liberty and human rights can hardly find more discouraging circumstances than where the military encroaches upon the civil parts of the constitution, and takes its exalted idea of what is due to its honour with it. The appearance of something of that sort happening in, of all countries, democratic France in the 1890s was the proximate cause of the most famous of all incidents of honour's kind, the Dreyfus case, a case followed intently in every land on both sides of the Atlantic.

The wretched Captain Alfred Dreyfus's own honour was the least important part of it. After he had been convicted of treason in 1894, the ceremonial stripping of his insignia of honour from him – the breaking of his sword, the tearing-off of his epaulettes and badges – was a necessary stage of his journey to Devil's Island. The official restitution of his honour with the final stage of his pardon, in 1906, never pacified the more implacable of his fellow-officers. Until his retirement at the end of the 1914–18 war, everyone in the French army knew whom you meant if you said that you had seen *him*, *lui*; and when in the First World War one of his relatives serving as artillery liaison officer with a British unit took to a neighbouring French one a request for support, he was formally insulted and the request was ignored.[5] What had happened to make such passions boil, to bring the Third

Republic to the edge of disaster, and to achieve such celebrity that Frenchmen and historians know it as, simply, *l'affaire*? Honour was at stake. Belief in Dreyfus's guilt, and unblinking fidelity to all others who believed in his guilt, had become a matter of honour for the bulk of the French officer corps. First, the campaign to reopen his case, and then the reversal of the original judgment – the righting, that is, of the original wrong – were understood to attack their collective honour, and to have to be resisted at all costs. Honour lay in denying that anything dishonourable had been done. From that position it was but a short move to fabricating evidence to make sure that what had been done stayed done. This was how Colonel Henry earned immortality. Convicted of forgery in the summer of 1898, he soon after hanged himself in his cell. From being a relatively inconspicuous figure in the case, he was at once made into a martyred hero by the anti-Dreyfusards. The public subscription raised for his widow is one of pre-war Europe's richest reefs of anti-Semitism.[6] The terms in which his deeds were praised by Charles Maurras are a striking example of the hyper-nationalization of honour:

Colonel, we are told by the newspapers that all trace of the blood which trickled from you across the floor of your cell ... has been carefully removed by order of the commandant of Mont Valérien [the fortress where Henry had been held]. But the truth is quite different. Know that this precious blood of yours ... stays warm and will cry out unceasingly until its spilling shall be expiated, not by you, in your yielding to such noble despair, nor even by Cavaignac's wretched ministerial clique, but – depend upon it – by your real executioners ... the members of the grand national union of traitors.

Continuing to address the maladroit forger as if, though dead, he still lived – a standard device of nationalist rhetoric in respect of historic heroes – Maurras went on to laud his boldness, his initiative, his self-reliance:

You used your gifts feverishly to deceive your chiefs, your friends, your comrades, and your compatriots for the good and the honour of us all. Your brisk 'Let's get on with it!', already known nation-wide, will henceforth acquire mysterious and profound significance. It is the word of a soldier, but it will become a word for the moralist and the statesman ... Your unlucky so-called forgery will be ranked among the greatest deeds of war, the only thing that was regrettable about it, its failure, being more than redeemed by your blood.[7]

Through the remainder of his life, which ended in comfy cohabitation with fascism, Maurras's concern with Dreyfus – a concern shared, it seems, by the bulk of Catholic and conservative national opinion – was not that he might have suffered unjustly, but that the Dreyfusards had, Maurras believed, done his nation's army dreadful damage. Its honour had been aspersed, virtue had gone out of it, and the sacrifices it had to make to be victorious in 1914–18 were the consequence. Whether Dreyfus had been guilty or not, in such a perspective as that, was immaterial.

In an opposite perspective, however – the *Dreyfusard* perspective which is most material to our theme – the question of Dreyfus's guilt was of consuming importance. If he was guilty, then that was that. But it became apparent as the nineties wore on and his name and case became public property that there were grounds for doubting whether his case had been fairly dealt with, and that the army, put on defensive mettle by external criticism, was more interested in covering up than in opening up. Hence the polarization of French society and the vulgarization of the issues, as every 'anti' movement and tendency in French life and thought climbed on to one bandwagon or the other. Men of honour became swamped on both sides. We need not believe that as many officers admired Colonel Henry as Maurras would have liked. We cannot believe that high-principled concern for the honour of the republic exclusively motivated all his critics. But it certainly moved some, and their interest to us is twofold: first, as representing a fastidious and elevated concept of national honour at an epoch when less elevated concepts were rampant; second, as adumbrating a supranational vision of honour which has become important in our own day.

To Dreyfus's side were drawn through 1897 and 1898 a distinguished group of Frenchmen whose belief that the soul of France (they used that sort of language as well as the others) would be corrupted if doing justice to Dreyfus was not held to be a matter of national honour. Of this group, Emile Zola was the most internationally famed, and it is probably no more than truth to say that his most signal contribution to the campaign, his piece, headlined 'J'accuse!' in the newspaper L'Aurore on 13 January 1898, was the most famous newspaper article in modern European history. 'Truth is on the march,' he cried, 'and nothing can stop it'; the legal risks he took in order to illuminate the dark corridors of power were only 'a revolutionary means of speeding the explosion of truth and justice. I have only one passion, that for light, in the name of humanity.'[8] At his trial for libel six weeks later he amplified that vision of the universality of the battle he felt to be in progress: 'The Dreyfus affair, ah! gentlemen of the jury, it shrinks to pettiness, it fades away before the terrifying questions it raises. It's no longer a question of Dreyfus, it's a question of whether France is still the France of the rights of man, the France which gave liberty to the world and which ought to give it justice.' It was a moment of national crisis, he declaimed. The nation faced the choice of salvation or ruin. It could only be saved by disclosing the truth and delivering justice. All France's friends in Europe were breathless with anxiety lest she should choose wrong. The military and political establishments, the popular press and the public whose minds it had poisoned, were pressing towards the abyss. Only the ideal of truth and justice could keep them from plunging over. But they, he concluded, were strong enough to win: 'I don't want my country to stay sunk in lies and injustice. You may find me guilty now. But one day, France will thank me for having helped to save her honour.'[9]

For Zola and the other founders of the Ligue des droits de l'homme – the *corps d'élite* of the Dreyfusards, marching under a significant banner – the honour of the nation was a bigger thing than the honour of the army, and suggested indeed something very different, something rather refined, noble, austere, and self-controlled. It was a valid and fine idea of national honour, but certain other, arguably less noble styles of national honour were, it must be admitted, more popular than Zola's.

The phenomenon itself is clear enough, though measurement of its degrees of development towards its climax about the turn of this century seems as difficult as to explain wholly how it happened. Analysts of modern nationalism more or less agree about the dating of the climax, throughout the whole of the North Atlantic world. An essential element of that climax was, simply, quantity; to put it crudely, there was more of it in society and politics, and it was to be found colouring more contexts, than seems to have been the case before. Much of it was drawn straight from history, plenteous provider of grist for the nationalist mill: the simple patriotisms and loyalties already going so strong in some countries before the French ideologues and German professors gave them a new look; all the memories and myths of the revolutions, conquests, wars of national defence and wars of national liberation, preserved and broadcast in schoolbooks, popular literature, and folklore. To read some hyper-nationalists of that roaring era is to read expressions of the faith seemingly so full-blown that one wonders whether subsequent development could make it any fuller or more fiery. Yet the next hundred years certainly did make available many new elements for such as were in a position to know about them or simply picked up what was in the air. Hegel's identification of the successful State as the advance guard of divine purpose and the proper source of its subjects' moral obligations was yet to come; Darwinism in due course would find its way along almost every artery of 'up-to-date' thought; the cults of instinct, passion, self-assertion, and self-sacrifice associated above all with the name of Nietzsche and his inferior followers; such additions to the mental furniture of the self-styled civilized world were all bound to work to enhance nationalism when they came into contact with it, as they often did. But the total explanation of this climactic nationalism requires the addition of a different dimension of contributory factors: the dimension of material circumstance. Circumstances now worked on the ideas like monsoons on paddy-fields. Democratic politics of course worked to articulate and spread national spirit; so did the popular press, now in its first flush of youthful vigour. Politics and press in themselves were value-free, but would naturally tend to magnify the sentiments most popularly effective, and nationalism with its blood brothers imperialism and militarism evidently headed that list.

The scene thus set, we may return to the one aspect of that fell trinity with which we have to grapple, national honour. With roots aplenty in earlier years, it now came into a blaze of exotic blossoms which, taken together, mark the most spectacular of honour's transformations. In earlier times honour had had an almost wholly personal application. The basic division made in it by moralists and lexicographers is between what is inwardly and what is externally sanctioned. Codes of honour by definition belong to collectivities, and an inner-directed idea of it has to have unusually strong roots, if it is not to be what the sense of honour actually turns out to be on most occasions, just an inward operation of an external compulsion. But whatever were the psycho-mechanics of it, the old ideas we began with had been framed in personal terms, extending at furthest to peer groups small enough to be personally knowable: the hereditary nobility, the knightly order, the officer corps, the revolutionary society, perhaps in rudimentary forms the Masonic lodge, the regiment, the profession. Such extensions were in a sense socially horizontal. More important had been the vertical ones continuing to find their focus in the prince, the fount of honour; the *ancien régime* soldier's direct explicit tie was to his king; so far as country came into it, it was in the person of the king; honour, in any case, was conceived of only in personal terms.

By the time we are now considering, the closing decades of the nineteenth century, that early predominant sense of the personal application of honour had been thoroughly collectivized. This marked a big advance beyond the revolutionary discovery of the nation as an object of honourable service at least coequal with the prince, where there was one. The nation was now commonly personified as a huge collective self. Some large part of the explanation of this momentous development must be the psychological one, that ordinary human beings find the quality of experience improved by identification with the extraordinary, the larger, brighter, and stronger than themselves. Analyses of patriotism and nationalism by social scientists always make much of this, and rightly so. We have already glanced at the kind of material developments which through the nineteenth century eased and encouraged such identifications. How fast and far they progressed from country to country is a daunting matter of comparative history which remains in the realm of impressionistic judgment. Perhaps German and American nationalism led the field. After all, Germanic *Volk* theory explicitly put the ordinary little German in his vast historic *Volkisch* place, making him – if he was responsive to that sort of thing – peculiarly aware of his nothingness without it, his all-but-superhuman potential stature within it.[10] American national theory, which had the opposite task of nation-building from scratch, made up in intensity and flamboyance what it could hardly find in race, history, or language. Just as the cult of the national flag seems to have gone further, faster, in the United States than anywhere else, so can be found expressions of American imperial virtue and mission earlier than the classic British ones, and at least as confident of divine backing. The mechanisms by which American citizens and German subjects achieved their respective identifications with the nation had to be very different, but in closeness of identification they could end up the same. So, in their own ways, with France, Britain, Italy, and the rest. Sooner or later, somehow or other, a common style of high nationalist sentiment suffused them all. It offered their peoples spiritual and moral as well as merely material aggrandizement through organic membership of their nation state, their collective self; it presented the nation-state as a super-person with all the personal attributes of body, blood, guts, mind, spirit, conscience, soul, and honour.

The basest layer of it was an extraordinary national touchiness and sensitivity, touchiness about affronts alleged to have been received, sensitivity about what in the classic code of honour were mere 'points of honour' and questions of prestige. This was the honour more of the swaggering squireen or man-about-town musketeer than of the responsible aristocrat or the chivalrous gentleman, a dislike as much of seeming to yield to another's convenience as of actually doing so, or of acknowledging error even if really in the wrong. Hence the quickness of nationalist public opinion to sense insults to the honour of the nation (expressed as often as not as 'insults to the flag'),[11] to clamour for revenge, and jealously to relish and protect prestige – tendencies of 'public opinion' familiar to all students of international relations and at their touchiest, it seems to be agreed, between about 1880 and 1914.[12] Hence the perpetual difficulty about international arbitration. We must remember that the nationalists did not have it all their own way. They had to argue against a well-informed, high-principled, and socially quite significant body of opinion forever pressing the virtues of internationalism, in particular the peaceful settlement of disputes between States by submission to arbitration procedures and even, in the years of the Hague Conference of 1899 and

1907, to an international court. Enthusiasts for arbitration could point to a substantial number of occasions when *ad hoc* arbitrations had worked and, by the turn of our century, to a certain number of bilateral treaties between States binding them to submit this or that class of disputes to settlement by the same means. Arbitration was in the air, no doubt about it. But it never got very far, and part of the reason was nationalism's jealousy of its honour: first, by insisting upon the exclusion from arbitration treaties of all disputes involving national interests and national honour; second, by finding submission to arbitration even for minor matters a crawling, undignified proceeding, incompatible with the pride and self-respect a State of honour should have. It was not only Gladstone on the British side of the Atlantic who had enormous difficulty in persuading Parliament to let the *Alabama* dispute go to arbitration; and when at last the tribunal met in Geneva and delivered its judgment in 1872, against Great Britain, the British member spoilt the moral effect by entering a not very convincing dissent from it. But what would have been his social and political fate back home had he done otherwise? Bismarck made no secret of his belief that no State worth its salt should ever go near arbitrations, and that Britain had shown weakness by doing so. Only with great difficulty did the German Foreign Office in 1899 persuade the Kaiser that it was consistent with his honour (*his* honour of course encompassing Germany's, by the old Prussian conception of things) to let his representatives at The Hague even join in conference talk about arbitration, although they all knew that it need never actually mean anything.[13]

This touchiness about national honour expressed itself also in a ready belief (a further borrowing from the duellist's code) that it required instant readiness to fight. A well-established part of the nationalist creed maintained that no nation was a proper nation unless it had fought to become one or to remain one. New nations, in effect, needed to be 'blooded,' like new soldiers, in order to become real. Whatever the intellectual or folkloric sources of this contention were, it became fully articulated in the revolutionary time, was given Napoleon's particular blessing, and sent swinging on its way towards our own century which has most recently heard it from the lips of those claiming to lead wars of liberation from colonial and alien rule. What was new about it in the late nineteenth century was the peculiar gloss of honour then put upon it by the spirit of the age. That spirit was, by any meaning of the word, militaristic. It relished war beyond the points of prudence and justice. Men who pile up armaments and practise warfare often say that they are only doing it to ensure the peace, but I do not wholly believe it, whether I hear them in 1981 or 1891; war obviously has magnetic attractions for some of us or some parts of most of us; besides which, history's record of the relationship between armaments build-ups and belligerent outbreaks is not encouraging. But the militarists of 1891, to do them justice, whether they were civilians or soldiers, were quite open about it. Their common belief was that war was good for the world. It kept nations on their toes, sorted out the strong from the weak in every context where they met each other, and made uniquely possible (especially for the young, who should most value them) the display of man's highest virtues, the warrior virtues, otherwise liable to decay in disuse. No longer much interested in the criteria of 'just warfare,' the purpose of which had been to minimize the quantity of warfare in the world, the militarists around 1900, with their Darwinian jungle mentality about the world of States, multiplied occasions when war should be unavoidable. The only ones we need notice are those founded in and around national honour.

Field-Marshal Baron Colmar von der Goltz, who ended a thoroughly successful military career as German governor-general of Belgium in 1914, was also an esteemed writer on national military topics. More central and representative within his officer corps than the flashier bogey-man von Bernhardi, his best-known book was *Das Volk in Waffen*, 1883, translated as *The Nation in Arms* and several times revised until its last edition on the eve of the war. Less well known but also thought worthy of translation was his book translated as *The Conduct of War* in Kegan Paul's Wolseley Series in 1899. In the second introductory chapter, 'The Special Characteristics of War at the Present Time,' he glanced at the power and prickliness of public opinion and the way it worked to enlarge small issues into apparently big ones, thus adding to the already weighty list of causes of war. 'Now that States and nationalities are in most cases almost identical,' he remarked, 'they resemble persons who would rather lose their lives than their honour.'[14] We may let Treitschke complete the thought: 'The feeling of national honour has become so keen and sensitive that we have clearly entered upon a new stage in the public consciousness regarding it. The idea of becoming Frenchmen is so terrible to us that we would sooner forfeit our material existence.'[15]

Alfred Thayer Mahan, an American naval officer and war college professor, became the North Atlantic world's most influential writer on the maritime side of war before 1914. This was partly because of the several good historical studies he wrote about the place of sea power in the rise of Britain's world-empire, but also because everything that he wrote – and much of it was about contemporary international affairs – perfectly reflected and reassured the power preoccupations of his own generation: pseudo-Darwinism, Anglo-Saxon racialism, imperialism, geopolitics, and a longing to be thought 'realistic.'[16] Having been the most chauvinistic of the United States delegates to the first Hague Conference, he felt it his duty to warn his fellow Anglo-Saxons against expecting too much of the second. To the usual list of reasons why wars would happen and why people ought not to mind, he added some specialism in 'national conscience.' 'The phrase "honor and vital interests,"' he wrote, 'embodies the conscience of States. Honor, or its cognate, honesty, speaks for itself; neither man nor nation should consent to that which is before God a shame, to do, or to allow.' Each nation's conscience would speak to it in its own way (has more extraordinary a parallel between individual persons and State super-persons ever been drawn?) and would have to be obeyed even if 'mistaken.' 'Even if mistaken, the moral wrong of acting against conviction works a deeper injury to the man, and to his kind, than can the merely material disasters that may follow upon obedience. Even the material evils of war are less than the moral evil of compliance with wrong.'[17] (But as to how 'wrong' could be identified, his meagre philosophy provided no clue.)

Earl Roberts was one of the most famous late Victorian soldiers. Early distinguished for gallantry in 'the Indian Mutiny' and with the Afghanistan campaigns of 1878–80 the best known of his later Indian exploits, and command in the first phase of the Boer War as his swan-song, he soon after devoted himself to the task of preparing his compatriots for war. The British people, he believed, had become altogether too slack and complacent, taking for granted the invincibility of their huge navy, expecting too much of their tiny army, and mentally inhabiting a fool's paradise in ignorance of what was happening all over the continent. His major speeches in the cause of conscription were published under the significantly borrowed title *A Nation in Arms*.[18] Some men still voiced England's old constitutional fear that big armies promoted despotism, but they were mistaken. The more nationally embracing an army was, the less could its force be used for anti-national purposes. 'Its very nature is a warranty of peace,' he affirmed, 'wherever peace is consistent with national honour and the sacred duty of protecting the Fatherland.'[19] Exactly what that sense of honour and duty might lead to was implied in his use of the conventional simplified version of Stephen Decatur's maxim. '"My country right or wrong; and right or wrong my country" is,' he told readers of *The Times* in 1910, 'the sentiment most treasured in the breast of anyone worthy of the name of man.'[20] He was particularly anxious to win to his point of view the boys of the so-called public schools and the masters whose business it was to form their characters. 'I would ask you, then,' he said, when commending the National Service League to the Assistant Schoolmasters' Association in 1906, 'to do all in your power to instil the spirit of patriotism and pride in their country into your boys, to teach them their duty to the State, to inculcate lofty ideas of self-sacrifice, and to explain to them that in learning drill and acquiring skill in the use of the rifle, they are doing work which will make them better men morally, mentally and physically, and create in them a stronger feeling for the national honour than, I grieve to think, at present very generally exists.'[21] Roberts's idea that nothing less than compulsory national service would bring Britain up to her proper military strength was contested by those who, like General Sir Ian Hamilton, the future martyr of Gallipoli, believed that it could be better achieved by voluntary service; but on the essential philosophy of the imperial nation in arms, they were at one. 'Voluntary service is inspired by the spirit of self-expansion,' wrote Hamilton, 'by a spirit of self-confidence so genuine and so deep as to engender a belief that others will be benefited by being brought under the flag. The spirit of Imperialism, the adventurous spirit, the appreciation of the romance of war ...'[22]

Adventurous spirit and the romance of war were rampant throughout all European and North American countries about that time. Not many were in a position also to indulge hopes of expansive imperialism. The imperialist carve-up of the world was approaching completion, as the predators (now joined by Japan) jostled over their last easy pickings from the moribund carcase of mandarin China: the episode which enabled that most maladroit of rulers, Kaiser Wilhelm II, to get himself immortalized in the dictionaries of quotations by likening the Chinese to 'the yellow peril' and his own countrymen, most unfortunately for them fifteen years or so later, to 'the Huns.'[23] Swaggering big-power talk was the common idiom of the epoch, and not just in the heartlands of nationalism or the obvious hubs of imperialism. It turned up also – which was surely less to be expected – in some imperial extremities, if Canada and Australia may be bracketed together as such. In each there occurred, about the turn of this century, an extraordinary crescendo of Anglo-Saxon racial patriotism and belligerence, which was part reflection of British imperialism, part parody of it. It had developed fast since Sir John A. Macdonald, only fifteen years before, had been safely able to brush off suggestions that Canada should rush to assist the rescue of Gordon from Khartoum. The mess that Britain had got into in its African empire was no business of Canada's, he said, remarking further that it was a pity that 'unreasonable expectations' had been aroused in Britain by 'the spasmodic offers of our militia colonels anxious for excitement or notoriety.'[24] By 1897 things had changed. The Old Queen's Diamond Jubilee in that year, with its spectacular military parades and naval reviews, gave the imperial masterminds a magnificent opportunity for suggesting the empire's potential military capability: Canadian militia and mounties in the processions, along with lancers from New South Wales and Victoria, and much made of Sir Wilfrid Laurier and other dignitaries from 'the dominions' who were present.

Two years later 'the dominions' were given the chance to prove their patriotism with blood and iron. The British government did not at first seek more than token military aid against the Boers. What it most wanted, and in the face of all other countries' condemnation wanted very much, was the moral backing which a spontaneous show of support by the daughter countries could prove. In Australia, at any rate, this was slow to emerge except (as in Canada in 1884) among the military, and the spontaneity had to be somewhat manufactured.[25] After the disasters and humiliations of 'black week,' however, imperial patriotism gained the ascendancy, as perhaps in Anglophone Canada it had done from the start, and the common themes of European and American nationalism were given strident emphasis. Here, for example, was perceived an opportunity for the new white nations over the seas to prove their coming of age in the classic way:

A nation is never a nation
Worthy of pride or place
Till the mothers have sent their firstborn
To look death in the field in the face.[26]

The mother-and-daughter relationship was worked to death as dominion poets and preachers, inspired above all by Rudyard Kipling who now entered into his fullest imperial inheritance, amalgamated the images of mother country and motherly empress. Local patriotism was good, but here was the summons of a higher and broader patriotism: 'For the young aspiring Canada ... the opportunity for ... achievement ... on a world scale.'

To arms, To arms, for motherland
    and strike the deadly blow!
Let crimson blood wash hill and dale,
    and stain the ocean's flow![27]

Considering the relative sizes of the British Empire and the Boer republics, this was a bit strong: but mother's honour was at stake. Lord Roberts could have been speaking for the imperial nationalists of the dominions as well. 'What do we care whether she is right or wrong?' declaimed an Australian politician. 'Our mother is attacked.'[28]

Out of such sentiments and of course a host of other causes came the great war of 1914. The enthusiasm with which most of the nations entered it – so different from the reluctance and resignation of 1939 – has very understandably contributed to make the question of its causation one of continuingly absorbing historical interest. To those whose interests include religion, ethics, and psychology, a large part of its fascination lies in its mixedness: mixedness in motives, principles, and results, and in the disturbing contrast between illusion and reality which forces itself on the notice of every critical eye. Historians like myself who have such an eye do well to walk humbly in the presence of the sacrifice of so many millions of human beings. But honour will not be gainsaid. Who listens for its voice finds it in the chorus calling people to that war and, equally significant, calling them to keep right on to the end of the road with what they had begun. The concept of national honour helped bring the war about. The concept of personal honour caused men to give themselves to it and, often, to conduct themselves finely in it. The First World War was in some remarkable respects fought honourably. And yet, the contrasts and the mixedness! Behind Britain's concern for 'gallant little Belgium,' her consistent calculating *Realpolitik* of the balance of power; behind Bethmann-Hollweg's confession early in August to the Reichstag of his country's affront to international law in the invasion of Belgium, his agreement soon after to 'the September programme' of German annexations; behind the generals, statesmen, educators, and preachers calling youth to sacrifice, Wilfred Owen's version of the story of Abraham and Isaac: the old man who would not offer up instead 'the Ram of Pride,' 'but slew his son, And half the seed of Europe, one by one';[29] behind his Entente allies' lamentations over the slaughter of their manhood, the king of Belgium's observation a few weeks after the beginning of the battle of the Somme that 'all these governments live off the war. They have an interest in keeping it going';[30] behind their talk about 'the war to end war,' *our* knowledge that it was to do no such thing. Yet were they all, all 'honourable men.' What else can one conclude than *either* that honour, along with every other key-word of high human conduct, was a hollow delusion *or* that, in some countries at any rate, it had gone badly astray?

3

Man and Mankind

THE GREAT WAR was the high-water mark, for the European and North American empires, of the nationalization of honour, a process that had been going on since about the time of the American and French revolutions. Within the past half century or so, the tide has somewhat turned as the consequences have been experienced of such a fragmentation of one of mankind's noblest impulses into the mutually exclusive services of the States into which mankind is divided.

For the military, the part of mankind which had traditionally laid most claim to honour, and which was still enjoying as much of it as ever before, this nationalization proved to be something of a mixed blessing. On the one hand were certain psychological and material gains. The sense of moving with the mass of a nation in arms was exhilarating; the quantities of soldiery and matériel made available by universal military service in the modern industrial state could be seen as gratifying; the expression of service as that of one's nation, people, State, empire, or whatever was not necessarily less ennobling than the old personal attachment to one's prince, and in any case seemed compatible with it. On the other hand the constitutional workings of that State brought the generals into contact with politicians, a species of men they tended to suspect and dislike. Some politicians, moreover, were themselves so suspicious of militarism that generals had good cause to dislike them. Meanwhile national politics were becoming stormy with the development of such deep ideological divisions between one party and another that the soldier who found time to listen to what was going on could really begin to wonder whether there still existed the strong simple idea of the State which came naturally to him or whether, instead, there might be alternatives. Honour, along with every other part of the officer's code, required unquestioning obedience and fidelity. But more and more the question was going to be put: fidelity to what?

Such a question was, of course, anathema to their military ethic, and it is clear that conscientious officers would do all they could to avoid it. In most circumstances a satisfactory way to do so lay in their vision of themselves and their army as the quintessential nation, preserving and cherishing the spirit of the nation within itself and sturdily remaining in being through no matter what political chops and changes. The Spanish army, which invented the modern military *coup*, was perhaps the first to discover the virtues of this theory, but what happened in Spain was of influence only in Hispanic America. It was the French army which pioneered professional detachment in the face of politics, wryly embracing the nickname of *la grande muette*, 'the great silent one,' an image touchingly suggesting the suffering servant, but in the guise of a warrior and, like Marianne, female.

From the French army's experience comes our first cautionary tale. This hard-won professional stoicism was sturdy enough to see it through the Third Republic. When General Boulanger thought he could crack it in 1889, he quickly found he could not. It survived *l'affaire*. Victory in the First World War gave it a new lease of life. The outbreak of the second found it still apparently intact. But by now the strain was showing. The Popular Front had given conservative Frenchmen a glimpse of an alternative France they preferred to avoid at all costs. To the general ideological tensions of the inter-war period were added a more bothersome succession of cabinet chops and changes than any other army had to put up with. The strain they had been under and the sand on which their code actually stood were suddenly revealed for all to see in 1940. There is still room for argument about the extent of the French army's will to resist, but not much. When Marshal Pétain, having become head of the government (16 June), within a week signed the armistice with the Germans (22 June), very few of the Frenchmen in arms took their cue instead from the eccentric junior and temporary general who from London (18 June) was admonishing them that France was far from finished, and telling them how the fight could hopefully be carried on. It presented French servicemen with an unprecedented straight clash of two ideas of honour. Their classic military code unambiguously required them to obey the head of State, the heads of their respective services, and the two most prestigious soldiers of France, Pétain and Weygand. Obedience to orders was one of their chief points of honour. One obeyed whether one understood it, or liked it; strictly speaking, it was not for anyone below the top links of the chain of command to try to understand. The aged hero of Verdun expected this obedience and most officers gave it to him. France, he tersely explained (it was of course impossible to do much explanation with the Germans breathing down his neck), demanded this orderly acceptance of defeat. Good soldiers obeyed orders in defeat as well as in victory. To give up when your leaders decided it was fruitless to go on was not dishonourable. To try to go on despite them was, and not only dishonourable but also, of course, criminal. General de Gaulle was soon sentenced to death *in absentia* as, simply, a deserter.

De Gaulle's line was to let the classic obedience argument subside to insignificance in the shadow of the superb demand that France now made of her children. He presented to his countrymen their *patrie*, glorious in the past, still able to fight the Axis in the present, and sure to recover full glory in the future. The armistice, he frankly termed '*déshonorant*.' What except low defeatism was in the minds of Frenchmen who danced to Pétain's mouldy tune? They had shrunk their honour to pigmy stature. *La France*, through de Gaulle, called them to deny that France had to accept a third-class seat in Hitler's new order. With the few compatriots who saw the situation the same way, he made insistent use of the dauntless examples of his country's warrior heroes and heroines of the past; in a particularly clever broadcast from Brazzaville, one of the first imperial provinces to be brought under the Cross of Lorraine, he trumped Pétain with Foch, sonorously apostrophizing him in his grave and drawing from his spirit explicit indications of where the duty of living Frenchmen now lay. Victory would restore to France her honour, greatness, and good spirits. 'Monsieur le Maréchal! In obeying you we shall be doing what soldiers ought always to do: our duty.'[1]

Not many French officers heard the call of duty as clearly as that, but all had to make up their minds as to what it was saying. Honour can never have had more anguished an airing than among Vichy's officers from the summer of 1940 until the winter of 1942. Most immediately crucial questions concerned the French navy. That Admiral Darlan's fine fleets should join de Gaulle was too much to be hoped, but that they should never join Hitler was imperative. In between those extremes lay a wide range of possibilities. Unfortunately, they had to be brought to a conclusion quickly. The British cabinet, understandably, however unfortunately, was in a hurry. Men of honour do not like to be rushed. At Alexandria, Admirals Cunningham and Godefroy after protracted negotiations came to an agreement satisfactory to the interests of one side and the honour of the other. But at Mers-el-Kebir, the naval port of Oran, disaster struck. Admiral Somerville anchored his fleet outside and sent as negotiator a Francophone destroyer captain who was also a companion of the Légion d'honneur. All in vain! The French admiral, Gensoul, was obsessed – it is not too much to say, unbalanced – through the tragedy of errors which followed by a hyper-sense of honour, aggravated inevitably by his nation's humiliating surrender and his hearty participation in that extreme dislike of the British which was so strong a part of the French naval tradition. Come hell or high water, he would *not* negotiate while British guns were aimed at him. He did not even take in precisely what was being said to him, a folly he was man enough later to regret. His behaviour offered a perfect example of preoccupation with national *pride* overwhelming assessment of *national inter-*

est.[2] Result: 1,648 French officers and men killed or wounded, mighty political advantage given to the Axis, no advantage whatever to *either* of the ideas of France in dispute; everything lost, in fact, save a certain sort of honour.

There was obviously much in common between Admiral Gensoul's sense of honour and that of the noble-born French admirals of the royal navy before the revolution, whose objection to bourgeois officers had partly been that, lacking the proper sense of honour, they would only risk their lives when there appeared to be some measurable national gain in doing so. There is some piquancy in observing that Gensoul of course was, like almost all French naval officers by then, of less than noble birth; the old aristocracy all over Europe had underestimated the ease with which their code of conduct would be adopted by the social inferiors who joined them in, or took over from them, the leadership of their nations in arms. The *crises de conscience* through which Gensoul and his like went during the days of Vichy must, indeed, have been at least intelligible to their German, Spanish, and Italian peers, whose professional military cultures had developed along similar lines. Not so similar were the military cultures of Britain and the United States, by whose more pragmatic (and, it must be admitted, sheltered) standards the honourable scruples of most Vichy officers in 1942 and 1943 seemed mere egoistic affectation. In the summer of 1940, excuses could be made for them. Psychologically, they had taken a terrible beating; honour being no longer obtainable in the normal way, by fighting for their country, they had to comfort themselves instead in not fighting. The true nature of Hitlerian domination moreover could only be disclosed by the passage of time. In July 1940 it was possible to have hopes which by the autumn of 1942 were shown as merely fatuous. The Atlantic allies, therefore, were not unhopeful in their planning of the North African landings, in November 1942, that Vichy's men there would easily find the way to join the side which now seemed sure to succeed, at no great distance of time, in liberating their homeland from a deadly enemy by now surely unmistakable as such. They were disappointed. Every variety of honourable sensibility was encountered, not unmixed with concern for status and personal antipathies, aggravated presumably by some latent shame and remorse. Roosevelt's long feud with de Gaulle did not help either. General Eisenhower, upon whose ample shoulders ultimately rested the political as well as the military management of the expedition, was frankly at a loss when faced with French officers who found so complicated what seemed to him so simple. He and they were not talking the same language, in more senses than one. He had in full measure his national military culture's high respect for honourable conduct, but nothing in that culture or in modern American experience prepared him for admirals and generals who found in their oaths of obedience to chiefs who were virtually captives of a national enemy grounds for shooting at would-be friends who wanted to liberate them. President Roosevelt's suggestion that the Gordian knot might be cut by putting Admiral Darlan and Generals Giraud and de Gaulle together in a room and accepting as Free French leader whichever one of them came out alive was impractical. At last the problem was messily solved but, as at Mers-el-Kebir, only at great loss to the allied cause. 'By the time Darlan had ordered the cease-fire in Algiers, Casablanca and Oran, the French soldiers there had satisfied their honor and were ready to quit anyway.'[3] Their compatriots in Tunisia, which strategically mattered most, provided no help at all; and the remainder of Vichy's fleet was in no more useful a position than the bottom of the sea at Toulon.

It will not have escaped attention that the nation we have so far had so much to say about was to be numbered, at least through the period of the episodes attracting our attention, not among the victors but the vanquished. This is not surprising, honour being one of failure's prime consolations. Although it makes success sweeter, there are more tangible rewards when the battle is won; whereas in defeat it may be the only reward that is left.[4] But, as the Vichy instances show, that by no means guarantees straightforward, unambiguous interpretation. German experience in the latter phases of the war offers an instructively different spectrum of difficulties, with a sinister twist to them.

Other armies may have been as much concerned with their honour as the German; none can have been more so. Its peculiarity, by the standards of comparably 'advanced' countries, lay in the inviolate directness of its descent from its pre-revolutionary sources. The Prussian nobility, once thoroughly militarized, stayed militarized. Even after it could no longer retain numerical ascendancy within the officer corps, its moral ascendancy remained unchallenged. Versailles, and the German army's reaction to it, made this even more the case after the 1914–18 war than before. An army of no more than 100,000 could afford to be very élitist. At the same time its leadership during the days of the Weimar Republic made the best of a bad job by ostentatiously emphasizing its apolitical role above party differences as defender (in embryo) of the German State and nation, whatever its constitution might be, while cultivating within itself two private understandings. First, its formal loyalty to State and nation through the constitution was understood to be due rather to something like 'the permanent substance of the German State and people.'[5] Second, since sworn loyalty to a thing or to a collectivity was to the Prussian officer mind much less meaningful than loyalty to a leaderly person, the army placed even higher stress than before (if that was possible) on the primary military virtue of obedience, with the understanding that, pending the restoration of monarchy or the introduction of a more acceptable constitution than Weimar's, this primarily meant obedience to the heads of the army. The necessity of such obedience had been painfully rubbed into them by the Kiel mutiny shortly before the end of the war and the near-dissolution of the army once it got home. That horrifying risk of revolution safely surmounted, General von Seeckt and the other restorers of the army's honour were determined that it should never recur. Adolf Hitler's assumption of power therefore pushed the army off balance. For officers sympathetic to National Socialism there was no problem. But the majority of officers were too conservative and gentlemanly to be sympathetic to it; they found the Führer vulgar, and really disliked the SA, which presented itself to their haughty gaze as a rabble intending to rival them. On the other hand, Hitler said nothing about Versailles, bolshevism, and rearmament which they did not agree with, and he had instant success in restoring their fatherland to unity, order, and purpose. Hitler, for his part, played the Reichswehr along with the same consummate skill as he used on all his potential foes. He emphasized its historic continuity with the glorious German army of the past, and apparently met with no difficulty at all when he plugged the leak in its code of honour by restoring its personal oath; what had for so long been sworn to the prince was now sworn unconditionally 'to the Fuehrer of the German Reich and Volk, Adolf Hitler, the Supreme Commander of the Wehrmacht.'[6] The circle of Hitler's psychological dominance was completed with the success of his manoeuvres to make that formal command personal early in 1938.

An officer corps so steeped in a tradition which, however abrasively militaristic it seemed to outsiders, at least contained a lot of Christianity, gentlemanliness, and chivalry could not wholly conceal from itself the nastiness of the national leadership to which it thus became bound. Hitler was not often revered by survivors from the old army, among whom notions of displacing him sporadically circulated through the late thirties before the onset of war and the accelerated growth of a huge, new, and more Führer-centric army made plotting to get rid of him so much the more difficult and risky. But what made the principal difficulty for such officers as were capable of thinking critically about the Führer was their code of honour. One cannot quite say, 'simply their code of honour,' because nothing was simple for officers whose fatherland, unsuitably governed though they might believe it to be, was locked in a life-or-death struggle with enemies on every side, one of them presumed to be red in tooth and claw as well as in principles, and all of them from 1943 demanding unconditional surrender. Nevertheless it was generally in terms of honour and their oath that Hitler's admirals and generals expressed to themselves, to their intimate colleagues, and ultimately, some of them, to their prosecutors the decisions they made about loyalty and obedience; and those decisions were, for the great majority of them, that it was their duty to go on if necessary to the bitter end. A few became active resisters, some sense of duty to a Germany theoretically separable from the Nazi party outweighing in the end the scruples inbred by their upbringing and professional ethic. The plot of 20 July 1944 marked at once the culmination and collapse of their efforts. Others, not prepared to go that far, at any rate peeled off before the bitter end came; they discovered that the personal obedience they had pledged to their chief might be slackened now that he had apparently become mad, and that their duties to their country and their own men could best be met by surrender. Von Choltitz was one such, who, after years of conspicuous and rewarded fidelity, found no good reason for sacrificing both his men and the city of Paris now that the war was, to all intents and purposes, over.[7] But such were exceptional. No darker shadow of doubt has ever been cast upon the value of military honour than the narrow, obstinately apolitical interpretation the bulk of the German officer corps put upon it: 'technicians operating in the void to the point of unreason,' as Gordon Craig has so well described it, 'but nevertheless Hitler's collaborators in the destruction of their country.'[8] Hitler's collaborators also, one must add, in crimes and cruelties unprecedented. Field-Marshal Keitel was thus convicted at Nuremberg. Soldiers and writers with a particular admiration for the Prusso-German martial ethic then and ever since have professed their inability to believe that men so consistent in their sense of honour could have got it wrong. *Generalfeldmarschall Keitel: Verbrecher oder Offizier?* (Criminal or Officer?) was the interesting title of Walter Görlitz's original edition of his memoirs and letters, the implication clearly being that if you were the one, you could not possibly be the other.[9]

But history has to observe that they could have got it even more wrong. The case of regular officers like Keitel was bad enough, with their stiff code of honour become so bendable that it drove them to obey orders and execute policies they knew not to be right. Worse by far, and worst of all, was the case of the SS, whose luxuriant code of honour, taken with extreme seriousness, drove them to accept as right whatever they were ordered to do. 'I swear to you, Adolf Hitler, Führer and Chancellor of the Third Reich, to be true and brave. I will go unto death in obedience to you and the officers appointed by you, and may God help me so to do.'[10] A personal absolute fidelity right up the chain of command to the Führer via, just one from the top, Reichsführer Himmler, was cardinal to the SS, its élite subsidiaries like, above all, the SD, and the army it so astonishingly spawned, never faster than in the last months of the war, the Waffen SS. The Waffen SS oath was (by the end of the war, anyway) slightly different, Hitler being proclaimed as 'Germanic Führer and Remaker of Europe.'[11] By the last two years of the war, that small difference was significant of much besides the facts that a majority of the Waffen SS was now being recruited from non-German-speaking peoples, that such men could hardly be expected to exult in the profound self-conscious German-ness which marked the original order, and that their motives for enlistment normally included, besides the anti-bolshevism which was common to all, some patriotic interest in the place of their own people in the Berlin-ruled Europe of the future. The larger and more heterogeneous the Waffen SS became, the less likely were its officers to share the entirety of original SS beliefs. Some even became ready to contemplate, with Rommel and the more cautious conspirators, the deposing (though not the assassination) of a Führer of whom it was sadly all too possible to fear that he was not the man he had been. In that respect as in others, the later Waffen SS shared characteristics with the Old Prussian military tradition, and displayed a capacity for detachment from the SS proper from which its apologists ever since have taken their much-contested argument that the Waffen SS, not much tarred by the Nazi brush, was just a specially tough, heroic, and honourable part of the German army. How far that was true is a question I am glad not to have to answer. (I suspect one's answer depends upon which part of the Waffen SS one is looking at and when.) That in many respects it had and deliberately cultivated a tone of its own is however undisputed; and two aspects of its honour-consciousness are particularly significant in our context. First, its relish for titles, ceremonies, rituals, and aspirations redolent of the crusading and chivalric knightly orders of pre-modern times. This was much more a part of National Socialist mentality than it was anything to do with Prusso-German militarism. (It also, naturally, belonged more to a pan-European movement and organization, such as the SS was in process of becoming after 1941, than to a simply national German one.) As good an indication as any of this aspect of it is the French writer Saint-Loup's book about the Belgians who joined the Waffen SS, *Les SS de la Toison d'Or* (1975): the cover, a dramatic image of frontally viewed helmet and shoulders of an armoured knight, no face behind the visor but a bright-glowing pinky-red fire colour, and a swastika-stamped iron-cross on a black, white, and red ribbon hanging on the chain-mail; the dedication 'To the knights of the Golden Fleece, old and new, who remained faithful to their gods [*sic*], their prince and their sword; who showed indomitable courage in the field and masterly skill in the tournament; who linked to those deeds their reverence for their lady, were unfaithful to neither their arms nor to beauty, and who feared nothing but the loss of honour.'[12] It is preposterous, and one would like to believe that it is not significant of very much in Atlantic culture, but it is perfectly consistent with the archaic romanticism of the Waffen SS. (One cannot but recall Churchill's remark, in his speech of 18 June 1940, about Europe entering 'a new dark age, made more sinister and perhaps more prolonged by the lights of perverted science.')[13] Perhaps in part romantic also was the second aspect of its honour code which demands notice: its cult of fighting for its own sake. Obedience to the end, glorious even if not victorious, was their pride, and in the increasingly 'hopeless' circumstances of 1944–5 they had plenty of opportunity to show how seriously they meant it. In this aspect, their code overlapped with that old army one, from whose hardening in the First World War it directly derived. 'The essential thing is not why we are fighting but *how* we fight,' wrote Werner Best, the future Gestapo director and gauleiter of occupied Denmark, in an inspirational tract in 1930.[14] Hans Buchheim points out that he lifted it verbatim from Ernst Jünger, author of *The Storm of Steel*, for whom such a belief had become vital during the increasingly hopeless last months of 1918.[15] Again an apt illustration may be taken from a recent French war-lover and popular historian, pseudonym Rémy, formerly a patriotic fighter against the Germans but now glad to be friends with them, author of *Compagnons de l'honneur*, and thus just the right man to contribute in 1970 an introduction to the French translation of Günter Fraschka's *Honour Knows No Frontiers*, a celebration of the great deeds of twenty-seven winners of the highest order of the Iron Cross, the cross 'with swords and diamonds.'[16] Remarking that his French readers may be surprised to find him introducing a book with two SS generals in it, this Rémy launches into a masochistic eulogy of their virtues, which includes the reflection that in a properly updated version of the story of the Crucifixion, the centurion of whom Christ said, 'Nowhere else have I found such great faith,' would be an SS Hauptsturmführer.[17] At any rate this revolting sentimentality is not narrowly nationalistic. Honour has no frontiers; 'there is but one fatherland common to all men, a fatherland formed by self-denial, sense of duty, and the spirit of sacrifice.'[18]

In the SS proper, on the other hand, the narrowest kind of national-cum-racial belief prevailed, and the nationalization of honour was carried to its extremest conclusion. It was the sinister culmination – one cannot alas! say the end – of a long process. Latent in the cultural nationalism of Fichte and Arndt, and of course in Hegelian political philosophy, the nationalization of morality was explicit in the popular nationalisms of the later nineteenth century, part of their joyful assertion of indelible national characters. How much it was seriously meant by those who liked to say it is of course doubtful. So much inherited Christianity and common culture kept – as it still may keep – men of different nations closer together on cultural essentials than their avowed national identities promised. The mental way lay wide open for extreme theorists to enter, and the fascisms which sprouted everywhere from the social debris of the First World War gave them their audience. So, to return to my regrettable namesake Dr Werner Best, a representative SS theorist, we find that his celebration of unceasing heroic struggle was entirely within a framework of superheated racial nationalism consciously striving to locate the mainsprings of a revolutionary new mentality of combatance (Hitler's street-fighting 'storm troopers' did not bear a Great War name for nothing) in a mystical concept of Germany deeper and more 'eternal' than it had ever been before. Part of this mental revolution was, inevitably, moral. The more perfect the knight of this new order, the more complete his supersession of those parts of his inheritance which inhibited absolute dedication to extreme struggle. Hence the SS's special cult of *Härte*, hardness; uncomfortable, it could be admitted, for the SS man who had not yet shed all the inhibitions of his cultural past, but the most signal mark of his virtue as a fighter for the only section of mankind which mattered, his own *Volk*. Maxims like 'sharp wars are shortest' and 'inhumanity now may be the most direct route to humanity later' were common enough among military theorists, and not Germany's alone, but in professional military milieux those maxims had to remain on speaking terms with a code of honourable conduct which partly contradicted them. The National Socialist milieu had cut loose from that, and if it was perfected anywhere, it was among the SS. Himmler's doctrine was perfectly explicit. 'It is absolutely fundamental for the SS man that towards people of his own blood he is honourable, decent, true and comradely; towards them, and to none others.'[19] The practical consequences of such doctrine are too well known to need exemplification.

With the SS version of honour, its nationalized line of descent clearly comes to a dead end. It was as corrupt and beastly, in a pseudo-military vein, as the Mafia's version in a pseudo-civil one. It was among the very worst manifestations of the malaises which had brought about the Second World War, and only real neo-fascists (of whom, in my continent and at least in the central and southern parts of yours, there unfortunately continue to be plenty) could regret its signal condemnation, together with a good deal of non-SS German militaristic honour, in the postwar war-crimes courts. But what could be done – what, to put it in a proper historian's way, has been done – to keep honour in better company and to make it again morally interesting to mankind at large? Let us glance at four fields in which, since the Second World War, and in direct revulsion against its most awful aspects, something of this kind has gone on.

First is the reconstruction of the old international law of war, and its starting point – paradoxical, like so much to do with the law of war – is the copious evidence coming from the Second

World War to show that though that branch of law seemed dead in some areas, it was still quite lively in others. Little of it survived on the Pacific fronts, and hardly any where Hitler's armies slogged it out with Stalin's, or occupying Axis forces faced resistance movements. But it retained intermittent usefulness on the western and southern European fronts and was observed to rather an extraordinary degree in the desert war of 1941–2. If any part of the Second World War was gentlemanly in the old élitist sense, it was that part, where virtually no civilians got in the way of fast-moving conventional forces: 'pure' professional warfare as near as you could get it. Field Marshal Rommel (he was raised to the heights after capturing Tobruk in the middle of 1942), although yielding to none in respect for up-to-date military technology, had quite old-fashioned notions of chivalry and was punctilious about observance of the law of war. This took him apparently to the moral point above which honour cannot rise, of preferring to risk defeat rather than to win without honour. The biographer who sealed his fame in our English-speaking world, his former prisoner Desmond Young, wrote that Rommel was especially touchy about hospital-ships:

Hospital-ships were a sore point with Rommel. He was indignant when he heard that the Royal Navy was pulling them into Malta for examination, furious when it was reported that they had been attacked by the RAF at sea. Drafting a strong note of protest, he was somewhat shaken to learn that an Italian general, frightened of flying the Mediterranean had taken a passage in a hospital-ship as a stretcher-case and had been removed, unwounded, at Malta. His final disillusionment came at a conference in July before El Alamein. Rommel was complaining bitterly about being halted for lack of petrol. Three tankers had just been sunk in two days. Cavallero reassured him. Other means had already been adopted to keep him supplied. Petrol was being sent over in the double-bottoms of hospital-ships! Rommel turned on him. 'How can I protest against British interference with hospital-ships when you do things like that?' he demanded. Cavallero was surprised and hurt.[20]

The Italian general was not alone in being surprised by such, it might seem, quixotic regard for rules in warriors otherwise remarkable for the ferocity of their fighting and for the fact that they were fighting for so disreputable a cause. Allied generals were surprised and puzzled by the same phenomenon, which indeed demands critical attention: the paradoxical phenomenon of such genuine respect for legality, such cult of chivalry, and such sense of honour in the army, which twice within twenty-five years lent itself to the most hegemonic imperialism on the European continent and, on the second occasion, missed every opportunity over ten years to avoid the Nazi stain. No wonder that so many German generals found themselves, after surrendering, treated otherwise than as the Hague and Geneva Conventions required; but not so much wonder, either, that some of them waxed indignant about it, or that their sympathizers waxed indignant on their behalf.[21]

The internal failures which had kept the law of war from achieving its purpose of mitigating, so far as possible, the hardships and horrors of war – much more pronounced after the second than the first war – could be summed up by the constructors of a better world under three particular heads: the sheer absence of it from areas where its prohibitions and restraints were evidently badly needed; the outdatedness and unrealism of some of it in areas to which it already applied; and 'the plea of superior orders.' It is the third which interests us, because the resolution of the problem has done a little to crack the shell of exclusiveness with which military honour had become stuck. Almost every serviceman charged with a war crime (I include ordinary crimes committed during war along with breaches of the law of war) in the post-war trials pleaded the pressure of superior orders. He had, perhaps, not liked what he had had to do – had found it distasteful, had suspected it to be unlawful, had felt his honour besmirched by it – but what could he do? Someone above him, the originator of the order, might be guilty, but *he* could not be. His duty, his interest, and, yes, in some respect his honour too, obliged him to obey. The war crimes courts of course could not wholly accept this, although they could not wholly deny it either if only because the British and U.S. manuals of land warfare had actually demanded total unquestioning obedience until their suspiciously timed changes in April and November 1944 respectively.[22] What they did was, according to some rough scale of proportionality, accept superior orders as a mitigating circumstance. This might have been interpreted as a temporary expedient, pending such amendment of the law as would couple the criminality of giving unlawful orders with the lawfulness of refusing to obey them. For reasons obvious at once to anyone who knows about or intuits accurately the nature of armed forces, this has proved difficult. The criminality of issuing unlawful orders is now made clear enough,[23] likewise the criminality of failing to act to prevent the commission of unlawful acts by subordinates.[24]

But that is as far as it has gone at international treaty level. At the last series of Geneva conferences to update the law of war, an attempt to legalize disobedience to unlawful orders failed. Something however has been done at national level.[25] Many army manuals, including those of Canada, Great Britain, and the United States, explicitly provide for such disobedience, and a few countries, trying servicemen for violations of the law of war, have expressly rejected the superior orders plea – I refer to Belgium, Israel, and the United States.[26]

A second way in which some recovery of a wider sense of honour may be seen since the Second World War is in an assertion or reassertion of non-military claims to it. The particular attention given in these lectures to honour's military and international uses must not, of course, be allowed to obscure the fact that, just as the idea had from earliest times lent itself to all sorts of religious and social uses, so many of its continuities and transformations through later modern times lay in fields beyond the scope of these pages. Our excuse for focusing so far on its military and martial uses has been in part the impression that those uses remained pre-eminent through the last century and well into this one, and that its other uses were cast in consequence into something of a shade. The military man's honour was taken to be the supreme sort, to which the others approximated as best they could; braving death for the cause you believed in was easily understood to have more honour in it than to brave life. In the *ancien régime* the nobility was accepted as peculiarly the estate, the élite, of honour; by the turn of this century, the officer corps of the armed services had with nearly universal consent been allowed to assume that distinguished role.

The First World War did little to challenge this assumption. The officer corps, at least in their junior and younger levels, suffered proportionately greater loss than any other part of the armies and their bravery had often been conspicuous. The intelligence and humanity of their seniors whose strategies and plans of attack had led them into such losses indeed was questioned, and it is probably fair to say that, except in Germany and the United States, the prestige of the officer corps was less than it formerly had been – especially among people who subscribed to the not uncommon opinion that excessive military prestige was one of the cultural predispositions which had brought the war about in the first place. But nothing that happened to the military's quasi-monopoly of honour as a result of the first war shook it as much as what happened in the second. The second, for one thing, was more of a people's war. This brought civilians directly into it to the extent that societies and economies became, overall, totally committed to it, though it is easy to exaggerate the extent to which this surpassed the commitment twenty years earlier attained in Britain, Germany, and unoccupied France. Much more novel and significant a degree of people's involvement came from the fact that civilians were now in the firing line as never before, and thus had every opportunity for the display of martial virtues on their own account.

Their experience may be divided into the two realms, bombardment and occupation. British, German, and Leningrad civilians underwent varieties of bombardment with, on the whole, an amount of courage and steadfastness which pre-war writers (military men, mostly) about aerial bombing had certainly not expected. It was in direct and fitting recognition of this that the George Medal and the George Cross were introduced in Britain as awards for bravery shown by civilians, parallel with and in no sense inferior to the bravery distinguished by awards up to the Victoria Cross. (It may be argued, of course, that civilians, not normally supported by regimental tradition, the spirit of camaraderie, or the martial ethos, need actually to be braver than soldiers to do the same kind of brave things.) Civilian behaviour under bombardment, then, constituted a case demanding equality of esteem with military behaviour in battle. But stronger by far was the case of civilian behaviour under military occupation and engaging, more or less, in 'resistance.' In noting, as the Second World War to an unprecedented degree compels us to do, the heroism and so on of resistance fighters – many of whom had no formal military background – it is important not to forget that the actually combatant part, 'the sharp edge' of resistance movements, had at least as long a 'tail,' a non-combatant backup, to it as any conventional army. Two aspects of the resistance movement's tail especially demand our notice. First, by nature and of necessity it was entirely civilian in character. Second, its members lacked even the frail and flickering title which resistance combatants might claim to protection under the Hague Rules and the Geneva Conventions. Axis occupiers did occasionally, in the ultimate spasms of the war, recognize the more military-looking of resistance fighters as lawful combatants. They were under no pressure to do the same for the civilians whose support, shelter, and intelligence had been essential for them. But torture, imprisonment, deportation, and death were the resistance civilian's fate, if caught, as much as his armed compatriot's. This having been generally recognized in the histories of the resistance in Axis-occupied Europe, the central field of honour has been enlarged to include legions of civilians defending their nations as directly as any military forces – and sometimes, as especially in the case of France, after their military forces had mainly failed them. We may leave them with a sketch of one of the least dramatic of them: Eugène Pons, a printer of Lyon, 'Catholic *petit bourgeois* but a profound Christian, one of those Christians for whom Christ is everywhere. Thin face, grey hair, big brushy moustache, blue eyes candid like a child's but shrewd and sharp ... He was honour itself, scrupulous in all his dealings, meticulous in the preservation of his honour.'[27] By clandestinely printing resistance newssheets on his little press, he braved death for many months, and in the end met it in the concentration camp at Neuengamme.

Another recent transforming tendency may be seen in certain shifts of military honour itself towards a wider field of humanity than can be perceived by the tunnel vision of ultra-nationalism, the service ethic of blind obedience, or the mere cult of martial glory. The occasion and pretext of these shifts has been the endeavour made since the Second World War to construct an unviolent and just world order: the endeavour specifically programmed, so to speak, by the Charter of the United Nations and the Universal Declaration of Human Rights, but sustained also by the soberly constructive mood which guided so many leaders of opinion as the guns fell quiet. This mood, so very different from the vindictiveness of Versailles, marked some of the nations' military leaders as well as their civilian ones, and was nowhere more significant, perhaps, than in its North American appearances.

We have not had much cause so far to consider the United States military experience, partly because, until 1917 and with the exception, of course, of that gigantic civil war, it was by world standards limited and peculiar: a hybrid experience and tradition, the Europe-originated parts of it undergoing strange adaptations in such very non-European surroundings. So honour had its place there, as of course it had to, but from early on it became more like a modern professional code of conduct than the chivalric and aristocratic-coloured European originals. Duelling, for example, their touchstone, was never accepted in the U.S. army or navy. When young Robert E. Lee went to West Point, a point of honour was actually to report hot-headed talk of duels to the authorities.[28] The Americans were very willing to be warlike, and did it, when they had to do it, rather well, but decidedly in their own fashion; their armed forces produced plenty of fire-eaters and heroes, but they did not dominate their tradition; a quieter-toned, more civilian-styled vein of leadership was at least as important.

Janowicz, in his celebrated study *The Professional Soldier*, summed it up thus: 'Regardless of underlying motives, contemporary [American] military honour repudiates the glory of war.'[29] This was to recognize the ascendancy, then anyway, of those military leaders whose minds moved in harmony with the internationalism of the post-war period: the Marshalls, Eisenhowers, and Ridgways, rather than the Clarks, Pattons, and MacArthurs. General Marshall stood out as a kind of saint among soldiers. The British chiefs of staff thought fit to quote from Pope's *Moral Essays* in their congratulatory message to him on VE-Day:

Friend to truth! Of soul sincere,
In action faithful, and in honour clear;
Who broke no promise, served no private end,
Who gained no title, and who lost no friend.[30]

No one ever thought of addressing George Patton like that. Eisenhower, Marshall's protégé, was also a man of mild and fundamentally peaceable disposition, who shared his patron's belief that war was something necessary but nasty, to be got over with as quickly and (within of course the limits of military necessity) humanely as possible; they were as far as could be from the enjoyment of war for its own sake, and took to the tasks of peace with conspicuous dedication. The odd man out in the American military pantheon was General Douglas MacArthur, who was not just flamboyant and rugged, as even more obviously were Patton and Clark, but who declaimed, at every opportunity in his long, successful career, his unique version of the honour tradition.[31] It harked back to those religious and chivalric sources which American professionalism normally left out of sight, and by the Second World War it was as archaic as, to take a very relevant parallel, Winston Churchill's romantic imperialism.[32] But though it may have been archaic, like Churchill's, it was tremendously successful; it brought just the right complement of passion and emotion to the other side of the tradition's civil sobriety to make the United States the highly successful nation in arms it so quickly became. To a nation at peace, however, MacArthur had not much to say. He was out of his proper element; his perspectives were only those of the battlefield; his judgment off it was much more fallible. A noble public figure, reconstructor of post-war Japan and inevitably commander-in-chief of the United States forces in Korea, he became political – more through impatience, passion, and vanity than calculation or design – took on his president, and lost. Characteristically persuading himself that he was in the main line of American tradition, MacArthur began to make the in fact revolutionary claim that the Armed Forces owed their 'primary allegiance and loyalty' to 'the country and its Constitution' rather than to 'those who temporarily exercise the authority of the executive branch of the government' – not a complimentary way to refer to the president, and not a safe one when that president was Harry S. Truman.[33] MacArthur was dismissed, and stayed dismissed. The United States tradition of military subordination to the civil power was preserved and, as if to add point to what had happened, MacArthur's successor was the very opposite sort of soldier, the Marshallesque Matthew B. Ridgway, who then and through ensuing years of sometimes acrimonious controversy honourably constituted himself a leading spokesman of the constitutional soldier's creed: by no means unheroic, but deliberately anti-heroic to the extent that it eschewed the rhetoric of glamour and glory. Thus was restored stability to the boat which MacArthurism had begun to rock.[34]

Anti-heroic also in that specific sense was the style of soldiering which appeared in the fifties and sixties in the service of the United Nations, and in which Canada for a while played so distinguished a role. Its years of richest promise were those of the secretary-generalship of Dag Hammarskjöld, the lands in which it was at times most nearly successful were Cyprus, the Congo, and the disputed borderlands of Israel. The immense novelty here was the transference of military honour from national to international ideals. The component parts of the several United Nations expeditionary and peace-keeping forces during these years were national, of course, but they pursued a peace aim, so to speak, instead of the much more familiar war aim. All their martial virtues and principles were applied to such strict self-control in the face of dangers and provocations as tested to the utmost their moral mettle and the adaptability of their honour. The titles of some of their books expressed their sense of the originality of their role: *Soldiers without Enemies, Soldiering for Peace, The Thin Blue Line, Between Arab and Israeli*.[35] The last title is that of the Canadian General E.L.M. Burns, chief of staff of the United Nations Truce Supervision Organization and then commander of its Emergency Force in Palestine from 1954 through 1959. Why did he take it on? In his preface he writes that the destructions he had witnessed during the war, by 'conventional' bombings as well as atomic, had changed his mind about war. He came to consider it imperative to establish 'some supranational machinery' as an 'alternative way to settle international differences.' With all its faults, the UN was worth backing; led by Hammarskjöld, it was worth serving. To the UN and its secretary-general, then, he pledged for the time being his loyalty. The other UN commanders write similarly; Carl von Horn of Sweden, for instance, and Odd Bull of Norway, Sean MacEoin of Ireland, Indar Jit Rikhye of India, and Michael Harbottle of Great Britain, whose continuing dedication to internationalism shows in his current direction of the British branch of the World Disarmament Association.[36] 'My job is impossible and insoluble. I dare say yours will be even more so,' was how General von Horn welcomed General Bull to the Lebanon in 1958.[37] All soldiers who have served in such forlorn ventures have found them more or less like that, yet through their reflections, as through the histories of their operations, runs the unconquerable conviction that, even if only experimentally, they were worth while, and that such could, given favourable political circumstances, become major opportunities for the exercise of the military art. The transfer of honour has been tested and proved in the fires and deaths of a long (and continuing) series of UN peace-keeping operations, the transfer of loyalty from the national to the international has been shown to be possible, and what international loyalty consists of may be read in the UN's Staff Regulations: 'Its key elements are stated ... to be integrity, independence and impartiality ... "I am not neutral as regards the Charter," Hammarskjöld once said, "I am not neutral as regards facts." A man has to have ideas and ideals. "But what I do claim is that even a man who is in that sense not neutral can very well undertake and carry through neutral actions, because that is an act of integrity." '[38] Of such may supranationalist honour be compounded.

The position for which the secretary-general pre-eminently stood was that supranationalism indicated, not a misguided lack of patriotism, but a bountiful abundance of it. This was to challenge at its very heart the nationalist doctrine of 'My country, right or wrong.' It asserted that man's citizenship was not only of that particular political country by which his 'nationality' was determined; that, whatever the benefits classically brought by the State (and perhaps not bringable by any other secular organization), there remained values which it could not master or monopolize; that, to put it crudely, man did not exist for the State, but the State for man. The fourth and last of our modern transforming tendencies is exemplified in those who have believed, with Hammarskjöld, that just as a personal code of honour might require the subordination of self-interest to something bigger, so patriotic or national honour might require recognition of interests transcending those of the nation or defined by it alone. That such larger interests exist must be clear enough in theory to everybody whose sense of values goes beyond narrow nationalism or updated paganism. The problem lies in moving from the free perceptions of theory to the clogged constraints and immemorial habits of practice. Like it or not, man's starting-point in any exploration of the universe around him is his membership of a State, and the better that State succeeds in doing the job allotted to it by Graeco-Christian-rooted political theory through two-and-a-half millennia, the more difficult is it to realize that the State, liberator and enabler in so many respects, can become a moral prison. The description of the forces and institutions working to that effect has varied from time to time. Sometimes those of the Church have taken the lead; more often, in recent times, those of the State, and most of all when it has been the nation-state, fuelled with the quasi-religious propellants of patriotism and nationalism. To break out of this prison, to denationalize values or (such being the only practical way effectively to support them) supranationalize them, has been the object of the internationalist ventures in whose company we approach our conclusion. At the heart of all of them is the belief that the highest sort of patriotism transcends nationalism; the belief that the Swede Dag Hammarskjöld says he inherited 'from generations of soldiers and government officials on [his] father's side';[39] the belief that the Frenchman Albert Camus expressed when in his 1944 'Letters to a German Friend' he wrote, 'I love my country too much to be a nationalist';[40] the belief that led the Englishman E.M. Forster to write, in 1940: 'when a culture is genuinely national, it is capable, when the hour strikes, of becoming super-national, and contributing to the general good of humanity ... We did not want England to be England for ever; it seemed to us a meagre destiny.'[41] These famous men were in the line marked out by Zola and the Ligue des droits de l'homme in 1898 and developed, more than by any other single individual, by Zola's fellow-countryman René Cassin, deviser-in-chief of the Universal Declaration of the Rights of Man nearly half-a-century later, world champion of human rights until his death in 1976, and winner of the Nobel Peace Prize in 1968. It was, he then recalled, *l'affaire* which had had a large share in forming the supranational moral sensibility which in due course bred his dedication to human rights, and all this, not from lack of patriotism but from superabundance of it. He fought in the First World War, he was among the first to join de Gaulle in the second, and de Gaulle's so much narrower, nationalistic reading of the meaning of French-ness needs to be balanced by Cassin's more generous one:

Je tiens de ma patrie un cœur qui la déborde,
Et plus je suis français, plus je me sens humain.[42]

To ask whether the one or the other is the more truly representative is like asking whether to give the palm to Joan of Arc or Montesquieu, with each of whom the history of honour in

France has special connections. It is neither in my brief nor within my powers to go back to that national heroine 'the maid of Orléans,' but to go back to the internationally minded sage of the Enlightenment is very appropriate. Montesquieu's exposition of the culture of honour was our starting-point, and René Cassin's understanding of it recalls the sage's confession of faith (which, besides, says much to a European Englishman today):

If I knew of something beneficial to me but harmful to my family, I would eject it from my mind. If I knew of something beneficial to my family but not to my country, I would try to forget it. If I knew of something beneficial to my country but harmful to Europe, or beneficial to Europe but harmful to the human race, I would regard it as a crime.[43]

Postscript

IT CAN BE NO condemnation of a set of three lectures on an ambitious theme that they left out a lot, but I welcome this opportunity to comment briefly on some of the more attractive and seemingly rewarding aspects of honour I had to leave aside. Books that do not set out to be definitive (and what book can claim to be so unless its subject is a small, dry one?) ought to invite further inquiry, and even to provoke it. I certainly hope this little book will. There is so much it has not dealt with.

The Soviet Union, for a start. Great was my surprise to discover that whatever might have been the extent of the Red Army's rejection of traditional concepts of honour in the first flush of the revolution, an elaborate honour system had come back into it since then and is now as alive and well as any in the world – better perhaps, than most. Professor John Erickson called my attention in the first place to H.J. Berman and M. Kerner, *Soviet Military Law and Administration*, where indeed honour makes many appearances: in the procedures for setting up courts of honour 'for the guarding of the dignity and honour of the rank of officer,' for example, and in constituting 'Insubordination and breach of military honour' as one of the nine main heads of 'Military Crimes.'[1]

The Japanese military's use of honour has clearly been so different from the European's that thoughtful comparison might suggest remarkable conclusions. Honour, to put it however loosely in translation, bound the Japanese fighting-man in the Second World War to do two things not expected of even the most honourable European: to commit suicide rather than surrender (hara-kiri) and to make bombs or torpedoes of themselves in order, supposedly, to guarantee direct hits at the cost of their own lives (kamikaze, etc.). Honour in Europe and its cultural dependencies has never required such desperate self-sacrifice. That, no doubt, is at bottom a measure of the differences between the religions and feudal ethics of the two cultures, but it also speaks volumes about the relative gentility of the military dimension of ours.

The anguished story of the French military's honour, which I had to leave at 1944, cries out to be continued through the Indo-Chinese and Algerian conflicts, which kept it a hot issue into the early sixties; so much so that I feel pretty sure that France must be, of all the North Atlantic countries, the one where the most has, since 1945, been written and talked about it. Small straws which the wind has blown my way are, for example, General Jacques Marie Roch André Paris de Bollardière's book about his reasons for resigning from Algerian command, *Bataille d'Alger, bataille de l'homme* (1972); Pierre-Henri Simon, *Portrait d'un officier* (1958), which fictionally traverses exactly the same span of ethical problems which tormented the General; and the documentary novels of Jean Larteguy about his army's travails, *Les Centurions* (1960) and *Les Prétoriens* (1961).

Turning now from countries to topics, I note with a little surprise the disappointment of my earlier expectation that it would be appropriate to say something, somewhere, about at least these three topics in the law of war: spies, ruses and perfidy, and prisoners' parole. The history of spying might be found to move in instructive counterpoint to my tale. When did spying become an occupation for a gentleman? It varied, no doubt, according to the value set on the people spied upon. The *ancien régime* aristocrat's strong sense of affinity with enemies of his own class made repugnant to him the idea of gaining advantages over them by spying. Something of this repugnance seems to have lingered on into our own century, but alongside it developed a more permissive attitude for which the way was perhaps smoothed by some equation of spying with sport. By the First World War gentlemen could spy without compunction, and even more so, of course, in the second. Yet did not some taint still hang about the spy? Instead of becoming recognized and applauded as the particularly brave and skilful man of war he usually was, his deeds never became as much and as openly admired as those of 'open' warriors, and the law remained as unsympathetic to him as it had always been. A remark of Hans Speier, in *Social Order and the Risks of War*, suggests why: 'Official military histories do not speak of the work of spies. The values extolled in nationalistic creeds are those of heroism, whereas the function of the spy in times of war is precisely to make fools out of heroes.'[2] Why indeed should spies be shot when caught, instead of being taken prisoner like every other combatant? The latter idea was mooted at the 1874 Brussels Conference on the Law of War and has been more recently touched upon by two of our age's most distinguished juridical authorities, Michel Veuthey and G.I.A.D. Draper. There seems to be no more reason or equity in current practice than appears in, for example, the U.S. Air Force Manual: 'Spies are punished not as violators of the laws of war but to render that method of obtaining information as dangerous, difficult and as ineffective as possible.'[3]

Parole is a kindred topic. No principle of the old code of honour was more highly valued than that which bound gentlemen and officers to keep their words. 'Parole' was the word of honour given by a prisoner that, if graciously allowed by his captor out of close confinement, he would not take advantage of it to escape. In eighteenth-century wars, officer prisoners seem pretty regularly to have been given some measure of liberty 'on parole,' and generally to have honourably observed it. No country liked to be seen to condone parole-breaking, and there are plenty of stories of parole-breakers being ostracized back home or even being returned to where they escaped from. Now, this edifying state of affairs seems to have died the death before 1914. How and why, I do not know. At the outset of my work, I thought that this part of the story of honour would prove particularly illuminating, and that it would be possible to trace its development in the law books. Great was my disappointment to discover that it had not seemed important enough a part of the law on prisoners of war to command much attention.[4] It is surely highly suggestive that, by 1914–18, officers were apparently expected by their governments and countries to escape if they could, and that parole was therefore not normally offered to them; whether because the offer would be refused, or because, though accepted, it could no longer be relied on, I have not found out. Nor have I come across any serious writing about it since Flory's 1942 *Prisoners of War*. In the 1949 Geneva Convention on Prisoners of War, parole simply was not mentioned. Is parole, for military folk, quite dead?

The law on ruses and perfidy also ought to be relevant. This has always been one of the most unsettled branches of the law of war. When does a legitimate deception become a dirty trick? Criteria must obviously change from time to time, and are very likely to be differently applied according to the degrees of respect felt by warring cultures towards each other. But no law of war can function without asserting the existence of this distinction and expecting men to be decent, brave, *and honourable* enough to observe it. Honour is of its essence. The deceptions, tricks, and subterfuges which come under the heading *ruses de guerre* have always been accepted, with varying degrees of good humour and resignation, as inescapable aspects of warfare; but the practice of them has never, to the best of my knowledge, been regarded as one of the parts of warfare particularly honourable to those who engaged in it. On the contrary, they have often evoked misgivings and been felt to require justification, even excuse. But never has a military writer in our tradition found any better excuse for perfidious conduct than, at best, mere retaliation. This is because perfidy is a deception not of the fighter but of the man. Our tradition with its earnest pursuit of prohibitions and restraints and its preference for peace does not allow any and every sort of violence in war, because it distinguishes 'the man' from 'the fighter' and aims to preserve something of the former even after the destruction of the latter. The law of war's fundamental distinction between combatant and non-combatant reflects this aim but only in part, 'the man' being present in the combatant too and claiming recognition as such when, for instance, he becomes helpless through wounds or sickness. War in our tradition does not aim to liquidate the enemy if his resistance can be overcome by less total means. Just as the enemy man remains to be respected when the fighter is *hors de combat*, so the man is there to be respected inside the combatant; and the reason for this, implicit within the law of war (it is only implicit because it was there, in the chivalric code of honour, almost before anything else, and what was so fundamental had no need to be spelt out), is that men do not cease to be brothers even though reduced to fighting each other. The key point at which their common humanity breaks through is in the respect they retain for each other's word when the values of that humanity are in question; in their ability to believe each other when it is not a matter, so to speak, of winning the war but of witnessing to brotherhood. A couple of examples to illustrate the point: it is not perfidy for fighting-men disguised in the enemy's own uniform to try to get past an enemy sentry, because the sentry ought to be careful about that sort of thing, but it is perfidy to try to get past him in the guise of Red Cross personnel, because the Red Cross can only do its impartial work of universal mercy if it can be trusted to do nothing else. It is not perfidy to refuse to receive an emissary bearing a white flag, but it is perfidy to encourage him to approach and then to shoot him, because that special symbol loses all its life-saving, peace-facilitating usefulness if men cannot be trusted to observe it. Perfidy, the breach of personal honour, destroys men's last ties with one another when almost all other ties have already been destroyed by their inability to live at peace together. In terms of international humanitarian law, it is 'the sin against the Holy Spirit.' The study, then, of the shifts and changes of its definition in relation to *ruses de guerre* is likely to be a particularly rewarding one.[5]

Finally, there must be a lot to be learnt about the place of honour among the revolutionary and national liberation armies which have made most of the running in matters military since 1945. A colleague commented, when he read the text of these lectures, that 'it was a pity I hadn't said anything about terrorism.' By terrorism, I think he meant more or less revolutionary movements for national liberation. Many people unfortunately do that, without pausing to inquire whether the violence used by them is terrorist or legitimate; and sympathizers with these movements have to acknowledge that, unfortunately, the circumstances in which they originate usually make some terrorist acts inevitable at their outset. It must also be admitted, of course, that acts of terrorism have tended to continue after legitimate guerrilla and even 'conventional' warfare have become possible, and have not always been as forcefully condemned and disowned by the law-minded as one might have hoped. Beyond those intersections, however, terrorism stands at a clear remove from the lawful operations of revolutionary wars and wars of national liberation, and need detain us no longer than to recall Samora Machel's observation that 'a guerrilla without politics is an assassin' and to note that, just as there are forms of honour among thieves, so presumably may there be among terrorists, the study of which by suitably qualified psycho-historians and anthropologists might throw up intriguing results. Much more interesting and important, however, must be the study of honour among revolutionary and national liberation fighters, by whom it seems often to have been highly valued, though how closely its meanings for them have approximated to any of the more conventional meanings sketched in these lectures, I do not know. In the only one of those movements and wars I know much about, the Cuban one, its meaning *was* more or less the same as for ordinarily chivalrous-minded gentlemen of our European tradition; which is of course not surprising, seeing that their education and culture had such largely European foundations. José Martí (1853–95), early leader and continuing inspirer of the Cuban movement, expressed his feelings about his people and country in terms different from those of contemporary European nationalism only in their greater sensitivity to the menace of imperialism – natural enough for a patriot faced with the American style of it looming behind the immediate Spanish one – and the element of positive cosmopolitan idealism which has remained a keynote of Cuban revolutionary thought ever since. To proceed from the liberation of their own country to assist in the liberation of others has long been a point of honour with Cuban revolutionaries, demanding all the same qualities of sacrifice, heroism, self-abnegation, humanity, and the like which the same code demanded of the more nationally conditioned European patriot. Do any other national revolutionary movements since the Second World War display as much awareness of what honour requires of them? What forms, indeed, does honour take among them? It would be very interesting if somebody would find out.

.

Notes

1 NOBLEMEN AND THE REST

1 Geoffrey Best, *Humanity in Warfare: A Modern History of the International Law of Armed Conflicts* (London and New York 1980).
2 'Since wars begin in the minds of men, it is in the minds of men that the defence of peace must be constructed.' Inscribed just outside the Trusteeship Council Chamber.
3 Giuseppe di Lampedusa, *Il Gattopardo* (1958); *The Leopard* (London 1960), chapter 5, 'Father Pirrone Pays a Visit.'
4 Ralph Waldo Emerson, *The Conduct of Life* (1860), in the chapter entitled 'Worship.'
5 G.B. Shaw, *Caesar and Cleopatra* (London 1908), act 3.
6 *The Times*, 29 October and 4 November 1980.
7 This excellent and often reproduced remark of Wellington's has been curiously difficult to track down. I am much indebted to Dr Hew Strachan for the information that it is to be found in a letter to Lord Fitzroy Somerset, 8 December 1845, a copy of which survives in the Sidney Herbert papers at Wilton.
8 Shakespeare, *Richard* II, act 2, scene 1.
9 Shakespeare, *Henry* V, act 4, scene 3.
10 Kim Il Sung, Report to the 6th Congress of the Workers' Party of Korea, 10 October 1980; Mr Alexander Haig before the Senate Foreign Relations Committee, 15 January 1981 (in *The Times*, 16 January); description of Idi Amin's purpose by a spokesman in

Jeddah, interviewed on BBC Radio 4 about 07.35 on 29 May 1980, and at once noted by the present author.

11 Montesquieu, *L'Esprit des lois* (1748); many translations under the title *The Spirit of Laws*. See especially Book 3, chapters 5–11; Book 4, chapters 1 and 2.

12 The reference is to Karl Demeter, *The German Officer Corps in Society and State, 1650–1945* (1930; trans. London 1965), 115.

13 A tragic echo of it is heard in the title of J.W. Zawodny, *Nothing but Honour: The Story of the Warsaw Uprising, 1944* (London 1978).

14 Demeter of course says much about it, but I have found little else besides a few hints in the long article on 'Ehre, Reputation' in Otto Brunner, ed., *Geschichtliche Grundbegriffe: Historisches Lexikon zur politisch-sozialen Sprache in Deutschland* (Stuttgart 1972–), 2:1–63. L.C. Green's *Superior Orders in National and International Law* (Leyden 1976) is the work of a jurist, not a historian.

15 See Prince Frederick Charles, 1860, cited in Demeter, German Officer Corps, 258.

16 Montesquieu, *The Spirit of Laws*, Book 4, chapter 2.

17 Christopher Duffy, *The Army of Frederick the Great* (Newton Abbot 1974), 203. In describing this general as 'a priggish, nose-to-the-grindstone kind of person who seems oddly out of place in the eighteenth century' and who was also 'a good Christian,' Dr Duffy's idea of that century may be thought rather unusual!

18 Thomas Gisborne, *Enquiry into the Duties of Men in the Higher and Middle Classes of Society in Great Britain*, 2nd ed. (London 1795), 1:273–4.

19 Letter to Major Malcolm, 17 March 1804, in Wellington's *Dispatches* ... (London 1837–9), 3:166–9.

20 Sir John Fortescue, *A History of the British Army* (London 1899–), 4, part 1:465.

21 At this point I must acknowledge a large debt to my admired friend Professor Norman Hampson, whose contribution to *War and Society: Historical Essays in Honour and Memory of J.R. Western*, ed. M.R.D. Foot (London 1973), did much to extend my grasp of this subject.

22 There is an article about this by Kantorowicz, of which I have unfortunately lost track.

23 E.g., Rousseau in 'Considerations on the Government of Poland' (1772) in his *Political Writings*, trans. and ed. Frederick Watkins (Edinburgh 1953), especially 176, 244; and Burke in one of his speeches on the impeachment of Warren Hastings, 1788–95. The key passage is cited in Louis L. Snyder, ed., *The Dynamics of Nationalism* (New York 1964), 85.

24 Rousseau, *Political Writings*, 153.

25 Ibid., 176.

26 Ernst Moritz Arndt, *An die Preuszen* (1813). I have gratefully borrowed from the translation in Snyder, ed., *Dynamics of Nationalism*, 146–7.

2 DEMOCRACY AND NATIONALIZATION

1 David G. Chandler, *The Campaigns of Napoleon* (New York 1966), 687.

2 Karl Zuckmayer's play of that title was however not published until 1931.

3 Quentin Bell, *Virginia Woolf*, 2 vols. (London 1972), 1:157–61, 213–16.

4 Although I am sure this is a true statement and am fortified by reading in *The Times* of 14 September 1981 that 'insults against the Government or the military in Turkey are punishable by up to six years in prison,' I must confess I cannot yet fully document it. I am very grateful to the learned librarian of the Institute of Advanced Legal Studies in London, Dr W. Steiner, who has been so helpful as to go through some of the main continental European criminal codes, hoping to find for me articles under which insults to the military must have been punishable. The results of our efforts to date are inconclusive. The military do not appear to be expressly protected as such. They would however have been pre-eminent among the 'agents and depositories of the public force / authority,' who always are expressly protected – they would naturally have been the touchiest of them – and officers at any rate could have felt themselves directly in another category of insults particularly punishable, insults and affronts to the sovereign. *The German Penal Code of 1871* [as republished 25 August

1953], trans. Mueller and Buergenthal, introd. Horst Schröder (S. Hackensack, NJ, and London 1961), Art. 96, specifically protects from insult also the national flag 'or any officially and publicly displayed insignia of sovereignty.' Geoffrey Drage, ed., *The Criminal Code of the German Empire* (London 1885), 134, says: 'In all matters connected with honour, the Germans still hold a medieval point of view; in fact the generic term employed by the code to denote insult (*Beleidigung*) is a translation of the *injuria* of the common law ... Under the Imperial code insult may be described as contempt deliberately shown by word or deed of the honour of another by one who has no right to show such contempt. Under honour is included the honour to which each is entitled as a man, as a citizen, and as a member of the class to which he belongs.'

5 Information from the late George Kitson Clark (1900–75) of Trinity College, Cambridge.

6 There is a good article about this by Dr Stephen Wilson, 'Le monument Henry: la structure de l'antisémitisme en France 1898–1899,' *Annales* 32 (1977): 265–91.

7 From Maurras's article 'Le premier sang,' *La Gazette de France*, 7 September 1898, as given in my colleague Mr Roderick Kedward's admirable *The Dreyfus Affair: Catalyst for Tensions in French Society* (London 1965), 41–3. My rather free translation.

8 Extracts are conveniently given in Kedward, *Dreyfus Affair*, 18–20.

9 My translation is from the extracts in ibid., 38–41.

10 Causing Schopenhauer to remark 'that every pitiable fool who has nothing to be proud of snatches at the last straw of being proud of the nation to which he accidentally belongs.' Thus Hans Speier, *Social Order and the Risks of War* (Cambridge, Mass., 1952), 48.

11 It is worth remarking that 'Damage done to emblems of sovereignty' was thought important enough to need a chapter on its own in Manfred Hoessly, *Die Delikte gegen die Ehre fremder Staaten* (Schaffhausen 1918) (but most of it completed by 1910).

12 There is even a monograph on *Der Prestigegedanke in der deutschen Politik von 1890 bis 1914* by Emil Wächter (Aarau 1941).

13 I have mentioned this at slightly more length in my *Humanity in Warfare*, 140.

14 Baron Colmar von der Goltz, *Conduct of War* (London 1908), 7.
15 Heinrich von Treitschke, *Politics*, ed. Arthur Balfour, 2 vols. (London 1916), 1: 202. For national honour see also 15, 29, and 73.
16 The head of the U.S. delegation to the 1899 Conference wrote of Mahan: 'When he speaks, the millennium fades, and this stern, severe, actual world appears.' Andrew D. White, cited from Samuel P. Huntington's *The Soldier and the State* in Russell F. Weigley, ed., *The American Military* (Reading, Mass., 1969), 125. Léon Bourgeois reported to Delcassé that Mahan seemed to be 'un esprit singulièrement étroit': Archives des affaires étrangères, France 2137 (1899), fols. 343r–345r.
17 Alfred Thayer Mahan, *Some Neglected Aspects of War* (London 1907), xvii, 30–1; the latter being from an article originally published in October 1899, the whole of which is deeply revealing.
18 Earl Roberts, *A Nation in Arms: Speeches on the Requirements of the British Army* (London 1907).
19 Ibid., xii.
20 Letter to *The Times*, c. April 1910, cited in D. James, *Lord Roberts* (London 1954), 447.
21 Address given on 5 January 1906, in Roberts, *A Nation in Arms*, 79–80.
22 Sir Ian Hamilton, *Compulsory Service: A Study of the Question in the Light of Experience*, 2nd ed. (London 1911), 49. In order to avoid the charge of unfair selectivity in my use of quotations here, I must remark that I know very well that both Hamilton and Roberts, whether they had thought it out or not, asserted that complete military preparedness made for peace, that Roberts expressed a dislike of 'jingoism,' and that Hamilton thought voluntary service less narrowly 'nationalistic' in its tendencies than compulsory.
23 It was in the course of remarks meant to encourage the German contingent in the combined force for the relief of Peking that he urged them to deal with the Chinese rebels as would have done the Huns.
24 From G.F.G. Stanley, *Canada's Soldiers 1804–1954* (Toronto 1954), 272.
25 This is the theme of C.N. Connolly, 'Manufacturing Spontaneity: The Australian Offers of Troops for the Boer War,' *Historical*

Studies: Australia and New Zealand 18 (1978): 106–17. Like most revisionists, he may be thought to overdo it, but his evidence from the papers of the British and Australian politicians and his careful reconstruction of the time-sequence seem conclusive. My main source for Canada is Robert J.D. Page, 'The Canadian Response to the "Imperial" Idea during the Boer War Years,' *Journal of Canadian Studies* (February 1970), pp. 33–49.

26 Cited by Barbara R. Penny, 'Australia's Reactions to the Boer War: A Study in Colonial Imperialism,' *Journal of British Studies* (1967): 97–130. See also her 'Australian Debate on the Boer War,' in *Historical Studies* 14 (1971): 526–45.

27 Page, 'Canadian Response,' 299, 304.

28 Penny, 'Australia's Reactions,' 111.

29 'The Parable of the Old Man and the Young,' in *The Collected Poems of Wilfred Owen*, ed. C. Day Lewis (London 1967), 42.

30 See Jacques Willequet, *Albert Ier, Roi des Belges* (Paris 1979), 115.

3 MAN AND MANKIND

1 Broadcast of 11 November 1940. (I am indebted to my colleague Mr S. Beynon John for lending me a copy.)

2 Albert Kammerer, *La Passion de la flotte française: de Mers-el-Kebir à Toulon*, édition définitive (Paris 1951), 162. My résumé is of the detailed story as told in that excellent book.

3 S.E. Ambrose, *The Supreme Commander: The War Years of General Dwight D. Eisenhower* (London 1971), 135.

4 For further reflections upon the peculiar problems of the French military, see the Postscript.

5 Herbert Rosinski, *The German Army* (1939; New York 1966), 173.

6 Translation borrowed from Gordon A. Craig, *The Politics of the Prussian Army, 1640–1945* (1955; Oxford 1964), 479.

7 Von Choltitz's memoirs are full of interest; *Soldat unter Soldaten*, trans. as *Un Soldat parmi les soldats* (Paris 1964).

8 Craig, *Politics of the Prussian Army*, 470.

9 *Generalfeldmarschall Keitel* (1961). The abridged English version is *The Memoirs of Field-Marshall Keitel*, trans. David Irving (London 1965).

10 My rendering of the oath, from Heinz Höhne, *Der Orden unter dem Totenkopf: Die Geschichte der* ss (Hamburg 1966/7), 138.

11 From Christian de la Mazière, *Le Rêveur casqué* (1972), interestingly translated as *Ashes of Honour* (London 1975), 68.

12 Saint-Loup, according to the Bibliothèque nationale catalogue, is a pseudonym for Marc Augier. Other books by him listed at the front of this one are *Les Volontaires: histoire de la LVF; Les Hérétiques: histoire de la* ss *Charlemagne; Les Nostalgiques: aventures des survivants;* and *Les Voiliers fantômes d'Hitler: l'espionnage sur les Océans.*

13 Same speech as is referred to in note 32, below.

14 Höhne, *Der Orden unter dem Totemkopf,* 12.

15 Hans Bucheim, Martin Broszat, Hans-Adolf Jacobsen, Helmut Krausnick, *Anatomie des* ss-*Staates,* 2 vols. (Olten and Freiburg-i.B. 1965), 1: 281–2.

16 French trans., *L'Honneur n'a pas de frontières* (1970). The British Library catalogue indicates that 'Rémy' is really Gilbert Léon Etienne Théodore Renault-Roulier.

17 Ibid., 11. My translation.

18 Ibid., 12. My translation.

19 Cited in Buchheim et al., *Anatomie des* ss-*Staates,* 295.

20 From Desmond Young, *Rommel* (London 1950), 158–9.

21 Von Choltitz's complaints, though hearty, are calm and gentlemanly; he understood that to some extent he was guilty through association. Conspicuous early British examples of sympathetic indignation are, e.g., F.J.P. Veale, *Advance to Barbarism* (London 1948), especially chapter 8, and R.T. Paget, *Manstein: His Campaigns and His Trial* (London 1951). Lord Hankey had something to do with both books.

22 L.C. Green, *Superior Orders in National and International Law* (Leyden 1976), 274–5, points out that, despite the unfortunate timing, juridical opinion had in fact been gradually drifting in this direction for the past twenty-five years, and that it was clear for all to see in Lauterpacht's 1940 edition of Oppenheim's *International Law.*

23 Each of the 1949 Geneva Conventions contained 'Penal Sanctions' and 'Grave Breaches' articles, reinforced by 1977 Additional Protocol Art. 85.

24 1977 Additional Protocol, Art. 86.

25 Frits Kalshoven, 'The Netherlands and International Humanitarian Law Applicable in Armed Conflicts,' in *International Law in the Netherlands* (The Hague: T.M.C. Asser Institute, 1980), 3: 289–335, at 333.

26 See, e.g., Eric David, 'L'excuse de l'ordre supérieure et l'état de nécessité,' *Revue belge de droit international* 13 (1978–9), part 1: 65–84, at 72.

27 Cited by Renée Bédarida, *Témoignage chrétien* (Paris 1977), 141, from Georges Altman, *Défense de la France: les témoins qui se firent égorger*, 1946. My translation.

28 Douglas Southall Freeman, *R.E. Lee: A Biography*, 4 vols. (New York and London 1934–5), 1: 53.

29 M. Janowicz, *The Professional Soldier: A Social and Political Portrait* (Glencoe 1960), 224.

30 In Fred W. Haberman, ed., *Nobel Lectures: Peace*, 3 (1951–70) (Amsterdam 1972): 71–2.

31 His highest flight in this vein was his last major speech, at West Point, 12 May 1962; it was apparently done without notes, says the commentary in Douglas MacArthur, *A Soldier Speaks*, introd. Vorin E. Whan (New York 1965), 352–8.

32 E.g., in the desperate early stages of the war which almost every high-placed person expected (and which Washington later intended) to hasten the shrinking of Britain's world power, Churchill's magnificent 'Let us therefore brace ourselves to our duty and so bear ourselves that, if the British Commonwealth and Empire last for a thousand years, men will still say, "This was their finest hour."'

33 Words from a July 1951 speech cited by Matthew B. Ridgway, *The Korean War* (Garden City, NY, 1967), 233.

34 See Ridgway's books, *Soldier* (New York 1956) and *The Korean War*, especially the latter, chapters 6, 9, and 10.

35 Larry L. Fabian, *Soldiers without Enemies: Preparing the U.N. for Peacekeeping* (Washington, DC, 1971) (this, admittedly, is *about* such rather than *by* such); Carl von Horn, *Soldiering for Peace* (London 1966); Rikhye, Harbottle, and Egge, *The Thin Blue Line:*

International Peace-keeping and Its Future (New Haven 1974);
E.L.M. Burns, *Between Arab and Israeli* (London 1962).

36 Harbottle's book *The Impartial Soldier* (Oxford 1970), xi, thus describes his subject: 'He is the soldier of any nation who dons the light blue beret of the United Nations where trouble threatens and peace has to be maintained or restored. He is the Impartial Soldier, and on his chest he wears the medal whose inscription reads "in service of Peace."'

37 Odd Bull, *War and Peace in the Middle East: The Experiences and Views of a u.n. Observer* (1973; trans. London 1976), 5.

38 Sydney Bailey, *The Secretariat of the United Nations*, rev. ed. (New York 1964), 27–8.

39 Cited by W.H. Auden in his Foreword to Hammarskjöld's posthumous *Markings* (London 1964), vii.

40 Camus claimed no originality for this remark, cited in his collection *Resistance, Rebellion and Death* (1960; London 1964), 3.

41 From E.M. Forster, 'Culture and Freedom,' one of 'Three Anti-Nazi Broadcasts' of 1940, in his *Two Cheers for Democracy* (London 1951), 45. There is a characteristically fine expression of the same sort of patriotism in (a very different sort of writer!) J.B. Priestley's contribution to Philip Noel Baker et al., *Challenge to Death* (London 1934), 305–21.

42 Lines from Sully Prudhomme, an earlier Nobel Prize winner in literature, thus translated in the Cassin section of *Nobel Lectures: Peace*, 3, ed. F.W. Haberman, 385–411, at 407: 'My country imbues me with a love that overflows its borders, And the more French I am, the more I feel a part of mankind.'

43 Montesquieu, *Pensées et fragments inédits* (Bordeaux 1899), 1: 15. After being introduced to this by the late Professor J.D.B. Mitchell of Edinburgh University, I found it also in J.U. Nef's pioneer classic *War and Human Progress* (Cambridge, Mass., 1950), from which I borrow this translation.

POSTSCRIPT

1 H.J. Berman and M. Kerner, *Soviet Military Law and Administration* (Cambridge, Mass., 1955), 50, 78.

2 Hans Speier, *Social Order and the Risks of War* (New York 1952).
3 Cited by Edward Kossoy, *Living with Guerrilla* (Geneva 1976), 90. He commends the sketch of the history of the international law on spies given by Walter Schätzel, 'Die riskante Kriegsführung,' in *Festschrift für Richard Thoma* (Tübingen 1950).
4 The only substantial reference to it I ever found, with the kind assistance of Lt. Col. A.P.V. Rogers, ALC, was in William E.S. Flory, *Prisoners of War: A Study in the Development of International Law* (Washington, DC 1942), 116–31, and he does not say much, though his copious references no doubt might set a dedicated investigator off on a promising path.
5 Those interested might begin with René Bourdoncle, *De l'influence des ruses de guerre sur l'évolution du droit de la guerre* (Paris 1958), and Dieter Fleck, 'Ruses of War and Prohibition of Perfidy,' *Revue de droit pénal militaire et de droit de la guerre* 13 (1974): 296–304.

Index

This book

was designed by

ANTJE LINGNER

of University of

Toronto

Press

Lightning Source UK Ltd.
Milton Keynes UK
UKHW012358200722
406167UK00001B/317